A Matter of
Personal Survival

Cover photograph by S. J. Evans
Cover design and art by Jane Evans
Diagrams and maps by Susan Marsh

A Matter of
Personal Survival
LIFE AFTER DEATH

Michael Marsh

*This publication made possible with
the assistance of the Kern Foundation*

THE THEOSOPHICAL PUBLISHING HOUSE
Wheaton, Ill. U.S.A.
Madras, India / London, England

The Theosophical Publishing House
306 West Geneva Road
Wheaton, Illinois 60189

A publication of the Theosophical Publishing House, a department of the Theosophical Society in America.

Library of Congress Cataloging in Publication Data

Marsh, Michael.
　A matter of personal survival.

　(A Quest book)
　Includes index.
　1. Future life.　2. Theosophy.　I. Title
BP573.F8M37　1985　236'.2　84-40514
ISBN 0-8356-0596-5 (pbk.)

Printed in the United States of America

Contents

Preface, vii

I The Case for Survival
    1 Immortality: An Idea that Will Not Die, 3
    2 Beliefs about Surviving Death, 7
    3 What Justifies Belief?, 13

II Objections and Refutations
    4 Approach through Analysis, 19
    5 Approach through Memory, 24
    6 The Human Brain, 27
    7 Evidence on Memory—I, 31
    8 Evidence on Memory—II, 39
    9 Evidence on Memory—III, 48
    10 Approach through the Self, 54
    11 Dynamics of the Self, 60
    12 Survival and the Social Web, 65
    13 Survival and the Brain, 71

III Mind in Action
    14 What We Seek Here, 83
    15 The Inmost Self—Thinking, 88
    16 The Inmost Self—Imagining, 95
    17 The Inmost Self—Willing, 101

18 The Inmost Self—Judging, 110
19 The Experiencing Self—Perception, 125

IV Explaining the Evidence
20 The Reality of Time, 133
21 What Kind of Survival?, 143
22 Extrasensory Experience, 153
23 Some Wider Questions, 163
24 Beyond Temporality, 167
25 Where This Inquiry Leads Us, 172

Afterword by Joy Mills, 181
Notes, 187
Index, 207

Preface

Death, be not proud. So begins one of John Donne's sonnets. The poet would persuade us against fear of death. In the end, a single great argument serves him best:

> One short sleep past, we wake eternally,
> And Death shall be no more: Death, thou shalt die!

How happy is this faith, when held so deeply that it carries one past the valley of the shadow of death, past the death of those loved most dearly, of those who don't deserve to die.

When I began the inquiry that led to this book, some fifteen years ago, I held no such faith. With Job, I thought: Man comes forth like a flower and is soon cut down. I then grew aware that the meaning of our existence cannot be known unless we face the question of death. I could not do so with faith, so I began an empirical inquiry. The account of that inquiry is what you will find in this book.

How plausible is it, wholly apart from faith and revelation, that the inner core of us survives the perishing of our organism? That question I pursued in the framework of philosophy, but I sought the findings of other disciplines as well. I reached a generally positive conclusion. This is grounded not on miracles but on a careful inquiry into what it means to be human.

The present book is not an inspirational tract. It is an existential investigation. However, those troubled by dread of death or by the apparent triviality of much human existence will find here, I believe, a strong antidote to despair and gloom. This may shift the mind from skepticism into reasoned belief, or reinforce a faith already held.

Apart from my empirical inquiry, those seeking a more complete world view will find an eloquent statement of the theosophical approach to death in the Afterword by Joy Mills.

Many people have helped me in the long preparation of this book. The manuscript has gone through several versions, and I thank all those who have read and commented on all or part of one or more of these, or who have labored with me, including Jude Dougherty, Sir John Eccles, Frederick Ellrod III, Viktor Frankl, William Gerber, Hywel D. Lewis, George McLean, O.M.I., Robert Neville, the late Wilder Penfield, the late Marius Schneider, O.F.M., Paul Weiss, and Allan B. Wolter, O.F.M. Whatever obscurities and errors remain in the work are my fault, not theirs.

For empathy and forbearance over these years, the laurel goes to my wife, Caryl, to whom I dedicate this book, together with my daughters Susan and Anna.

I

The Case for Survival

1

Immortality: An Idea that Will Not Die

Can a plausible naturalistic case be made for personal survival after death? That is the question this book will examine. To many, such an enterprise will seem irrational. Those who feel that survival is nonsense, an illusion, a superstition, form a large and glittering company. They include much of the world's intellectual establishment, though by no means all of it. Their accepted wisdom holds to a reductionist world view. In this reductionist view humans are basically nothing but complex animal organisms; organisms are nothing but temporarily organized matter; our earth is nothing but a speck in a heedless immensity of galaxies hurtling outward in space-time. In this light the idea of immortality—of personal survival after death—becomes not only foolish but taboo, undiscussable, among many of those who set the *Zeitgeist*.

And yet the idea refuses to die.

Public opinion polls find over two-thirds of Americans saying that they believe in life after death.[1] A varying but substantial number of Western Europeans affirm the same. And survival once again is being mentioned in public. Its taboo is slipping. Saul Bellow, a Nobel laureate, has run a theme of immortality through his novel *Humboldt's Gift*. Accounts of "near-death experiences," supposed post-mortem encounters, have sold in the millions. The nation's best-known expert on death and dying, Dr. Elisabeth Kübler-Ross, declares: "I know for a fact there is life after death."[2]

Many clearly yearn for the hope and consolation of believing in survival, both for their loved ones and for themselves. Many cling to the Christian promise. But those who do so meet with discouragement. The poet Richard Eberhart voices the feelings of many:

> Not through the rational mind,
> But by elation coming to me
> Sometimes, I am sure
> Death is but a door . . . .
>
> Perhaps it is only human need.
> When reason rules, reason denies it.
> But comes elation unto me
> And blows God all through me.[3]

But how can a solid belief, today, be grounded on simple elation? The feeling of cognitive dissonance grows. Beliefs shrink to half-beliefs and then wither into husks. Among educated people, the old sense of what life means has often vanished. "There is no doubt," writes psychiatrist Viktor Frankl, "that the existential vacuum is increasing and spreading."[4] This recalls a prediction made many years ago by William McDougall, one of the founders of social psychology. In 1911, introducing his book *Body and Mind,* McDougall predicted that belief in life after death would dwindle "if science should continue to maintain the mechanistic dogma." And that, he warned, might be socially calamitous, "for every vigorous nation seems to have possessed this belief, and the loss of it has accompanied the decay of national vigor in many instances."[5] In 1971, sixty years and much history later, the rebellious Yugoslav writer Mihajlo Mihajlov suggested:

> Never before has the question of personal immortality been posed as sharply before each man—not theoretically but practically—as in the present totalitarian societies. If physical death is the end, then (submission to) slavery is justified. Then, it is indeed better to be a living slave carrying out unquestioning the directions of the party than not to be. And vice

versa—if the soul, the 'I' of each of us, is immortal, then worship of outside violence is the loss of the soul, which is worse than the loss of life. Thus in totalitarian societies one can observe the rebirth of religious life which the nineteenth century seemed to have completely rejected.[6]

Whatever the social value of believing in survival, its immediate importance lies at the personal level. First of all, as Mihajlov suggests, this belief—if it is truly direct and deep—can give a new foundation to one's life. It carries one beyond servility, beyond dependence on political or other dogmas, beyond the power of any autocrat. This belief enables one to obey a different voice, none other than one's own enduring voice—inspired perhaps by a still deeper universal voice. This founds one's life in quite a new way.

The present inquiry will seek to allay, or even end, the cognitive dissonance about survival by treating this belief as an empirical hypothesis like any other. We shall not consider it from the standpoint of miracle or revelation but from the standpoint of an existential claim about what it is to be human in the real world. This is by no means the only method for coming to a firm belief in survival after death. Such a belief may grow out of simple yearning, out of one's religious faith, or out of one's philosophic faith—that is, out of a metaphysics reached on other grounds than an empirical inquiry into the nature of being-human. I would not denigrate these other routes, but they are not the path chosen here. Our present inquiry, using the tools of science and philosophy, will—if successful—reinforce and solidify one's belief in survival no matter what one's original grounds for hoping or affirming life after death.

Specifically, our survival hypothesis asserts that human beings experience indefinite continuation of their self-identity beyond physical death. This we shall call the full-life hypothesis. This personal state should be distinguished from objective immortality, that is, merging of one's identity into the All, the Absolute, Brahman, Nirvana, the Life Force, Evolution, Humanity, the Proletariat, or God under any other name. Many people who scoff at the notion of personal survival believe in some form of objective immortality. We distinguish our hypothesis also from referential immortality, the notion that one survives death in the memory of one's family and friends or in the works one leaves behind: that view, so far as it goes, seems a truism. Personal survival could, by miracle, include resurrection of one's biological organism; but there seem to be no naturalistic grounds for expecting this. Also, as St. Paul affirmed, the Christian view of resurrection involves not a natural body but a spiritual body (I Corinthians 15:44). Thus, whenever in this inquiry the words *survival,* or *immortality,* or *life after death* are used, unless otherwise indicated they mean personal survival, that is, indefinite continuation of one's self-identity beyond the death of one's organism.

Our procedure will be as follows: First, we shall cast a glance back at the history of human beliefs about survival after death. Then we shall consider the proper methodology for use in this inquiry. In Part Two, we shall examine various objections—both analytic ones and empirical ones—that have been raised against the survival hypothesis, and the arguments and evidence that may counteract them. In Part Three, we shall inquire into activities of the mind that are not plausibly reducible to brain function. Finally, in Part Four, we shall seek out a defensible ontology—a view as to the fundamental structure of reality—that can explain the evidence and open the way to personal survival.

2

Beliefs about Surviving Death

In most human cultures a belief in survival seems to have been held as normal and natural, in contrast to the situation today. Anthropologist Cottie Burland, ranging widely among primitive societies, found many varied stories about the fate of the soul, but concluded that "the simple belief in survival is archetypal and built into the human personality."[1] This is doubtless reinforced, Burland suggests, by the widespread experience that the dead can reappear as ghosts. No culture has been found, he reports, "in which specially gifted individuals are not able to fall into trance and converse with disembodied souls."

Moreover, as J. G. Frazer pointed out in his classic survey, one of the landmarks of early anthropology, the appearance of dead people in dreams leads "the savage" to infer that these people still exist somewhere and somehow apart from their bodies. Primitive man deduces that such ghosts can help or harm him in daily life, as they seem to do in dreams, and he must therefore propitiate and even worship them. This fits without cognitive dissonance into the primitive animistic view of nature, with natural events caused by personified spirits. Frazer concludes that "belief in the survival of the human spirit after death is world-wide; it is found among men in all stages of culture from the lowest to the highest."[2]

Burial customs suggest that belief in survival is very old. Even the Neanderthals of 80,000 years ago buried joints of meat along with their dead.[3] That required a sacrifice of food of substantial value. It seems to imply that they believed in an after-life. Some burial behavior has also been observed among elephants, chimpanzees, baboons, and even ants.[4] However, that may be simply a form of grieving (or, among the ants, social sanitation) rather than expectation of an after-life, as with humans.

Some form of belief in survival has also marked most higher cultures, or civilizations. For them survival has been the accepted and established view as part of their religion. In India the Hindu doctrine holds that each soul is reborn many times. The new birth, in human or animal form, depends on one's conduct in previous incarnations. Similar views are held by Buddhists and Jainists. Eventually the round of births may be ended and the soul released, either to merge with the Absolute (Brahman or Nirvana) or, in some versions, to enter more personal heavens or hells.[5]

Ancient Babylonian myths of Gilgamesh, Adapa, and Aghat tell of possible immortality, like that of the gods, but in such discouraging terms that the heroes reject it. In Egypt Pharaohs and wealthy nobles could become happily immortal, a view modeled on the death and resurrection of the god Osiris. This privilege reportedly became far more widespread in later Pharaonic times, after 2,000 B.C., together with a judgment by Osiris of the dead person.[6]

In Central America the Aztecs had three paradises where specific groups would go, but all others faced a hellish journey to the north after death, finally arriving at a dark oblivion. In South America the Inca culture, like the Egyptians, mummified their corpses. They also, according to the Jesuit Blas Valera, prayed to their gods to "look after the dead man, not to let his body be spoiled and lost in the earth, not to allow his soul to wander but to gather it in and keep it in some region of happiness."[7]

China, with the world's oldest continuous civilization, has had varied and rich religious beliefs, including Confucianism,

Taoism, and Buddhism. Apart from ancestor worship, however, the main Chinese thrust for personal immortality appears to have expressed itself in popular Taoism. For centuries Taoist priests peddled magical potions and techniques for attaining endless life.[8]

In the seventh century B.C. the prophet Zoroaster (Zarathustra), whose views spread widely in the Persian empire, introduced the idea of a last judgment on all humans, dead and alive, at a particular time, with the righteous going to paradise across a narrow bridge and the wicked falling into molten metal.

Among the ancient Hebrews the dead persisted in Sheol, a vast underground cavern or pit, a place—in Job's words —"of gloom and chaos, where light is as darkness" (Job 10:22). The early Greeks devised a similar joyless habitation for the shades of the dead, in Erebus or Hades. Later both cultures developed a belief in desirable immortality. They joined this with a divine judgment of the dead, leading to happy resurrection for the justified and hellish torments for the wicked. These views spread among Hebrews and Greeks after about 600 B.C., perhaps influenced by the Zoroastrians.

Some historians suggest that these last notions emerged along with the idea of autonomous, responsible individuals, contrasting with an earlier tribal or civic focus. The resurrection belief spread among the Hebrews, especially after 300 B.C. It was a dominant view at the time of Jesus, espoused by the Pharisees, though disputed by the traditionalist Sadducees. Among the Greeks the idea of a blessed after-life spread through the mystery cults—the Eleusinian, then the Dionysian and Orphic, mysteries. Plato, in argument and myth, affirmed the soul's survival in the eternal realm; he also espoused the notion of rebirths. Aristotle, by contrast, seems to have believed that only the impersonal mind in us is eternal.[9]

Jesus preached eternal life for those who believe in him, together with an imminent last judgment, consigning some to blessed resurrection and others to damnation. Paul the Apostle, organizer of Christianity, stressed above all the promise of eternal life for followers of Christ through faith and by grace, with resurrection of the (spiritual) body. As sign and proof of this "foolish" doctrine, Paul pointed to the actual resurrection of Jesus himself. Nor did he neglect the theme of last judgment. These three themes—eternal life for the faithful, resurrection, and last judgment—have echoed down the centuries of Christendom. Different eras, sects, and leaders have interpreted the themes differently, but all of them survive today.[10]

Meanwhile, the newest world religion, Islam, emerged from Arabian oases in the seventh century after Christ. Islam's prophet, Mohammed, like his predecessors, preached eternal life for the faithful. His word from God included a final judgment assigning the righteous to a lush paradise attended by "large-eyed houris like unto hidden pearls," while the wicked roast in hell.[11]

Along with these widespread beliefs in survival, contrary views made headway among the sophisticated during at least two periods of world history. These periods are: (1) the height of the Greco-Roman era, and (2) the height of our own culture since the Renaissance. Both Epicureanism and Stoicism, though they originated fairly early, seem to have flourished especially at the peak of Rome's power and glory: a time when the old gods and old civism could not stave off cynicism and boredom among the upper class. These philosophies differ in various ways, including their ontologies. Epicureans were atomists, reducing the world to dissolvable combinations of atoms. The Stoics held that God or creative fire brings about identical recurring world-cycles, in one of which we live, playing our short and predetermined roles. For both philosophies, the goal is to face life's disasters and duties with equanimity (for the Epicureans, tranquility; for the Stoics, apathy), thus overcoming fear of death. The Epicureans especially argue that death is oblivion and that this knowledge liberates. Lucretius in his great poem writes:

> For thou shalt sleep, and never wake again,
> And quitting life, shalt quit thy living pain . . .
> The worst that can befall thee, measured right,
> Is a sound slumber, and a long good-night . . .

For all the dismal tales, that poets tell
Are verified on earth, and not in hell.[12]

The Stoics, more varied in their views, sought above all to conquer fear of death. Thus the philosopher-emperor Marcus Aurelius wrote:

> What, then, is that which is able to conduct a man? One thing and one only—Philosophy. But this consists in keeping the daemon within a man free from violence and unharmed, superior to pains and pleasure . . . accepting all that happens and all that is allotted . . . and finally, waiting for death with a cheerful mind, as being nothing else than a dissolution of the elements of which every living being is compounded.[13]

Such a welcome for death, occurring at the peak of a society's power and wealth, found an echo among some tender-minded souls in the nineteenth and twentieth centuries. But the crucial trend among us that has weakened survival beliefs is the spread of a mechanistic world-view.

The mechanistic view—the world as intricate machine—swept forward in the past several centuries in tandem with two other great movements: the focus on man as the measure (instead of God), and the effort to understand and use nature through exploration and experiment (instead of relying on authority and tradition). These three trends brought a revolution in human knowledge, immense progress, and a sense of liberation to many. Of the three the mechanistic view of the world probably did most damage to survival ideas. This mechanistic model spread from physics and chemistry into physiology and psychology. By the end of the nineteenth century, mechanistic explanation had largely driven from intellectual respectability not only primitive animism but also sophisticated animism—the view that meaningful purpose plays some irreducible role in nature and especially in humans. By then, as McDougall reports, such a view of "the psychophysical problem" was generally regarded in academic circles as finally driven from the field.[14] Survival beliefs simply did not fit into the mechanistic world-view, which sees human existence as grounded solely in physiochemical events. Survival had changed from being a normal and natural belief to an irrational wish-fulfillment or supernatural miracle.

Along with mechanism's triumph, the spirit of the times began to darken. In 1903 Bertrand Russell gave noble voice to this ontological darkness:

> That Man is the product of causes which had no prevision of the end they were achieving; that his origin, his growth, his hopes and fears, his loves and his beliefs, are but the outcome of accidental collocations of atoms; that no fire, no heroism, no intensity of thought and feeling, can preserve an individual life beyond the grave; that all the labours of the ages, all the devotion, all the inspiration, all the noonday brightness of human genius, are destined to extinction in the vast death of the solar system, and that the whole temple of Man's achievements must inevitably be buried beneath the debris of a universe in ruins—all these things, if not quite beyond dispute, are yet so nearly certain, that no philosophy which rejects them can hope to stand. Only within the scaffolding of these truths, only on the firm foundation of unyielding despair, can the soul's habitation henceforth be safely built.[15]

Social calamities of the twentieth century added further notes of gloom to these ontological ones. At the same time, developments in various disciplines, including physics, physiology, psychology, and philosophy, began to challenge mechanistic reductionism in our century. They have not so far overthrown it. Also, certain events continue to be reported that are inexplicable under a reductionist view of human nature. These include accounts of extrasensory perception, return from death, reincarnation, and communication with dead persons. We shall consider later how much weight to give such reports.

Meanwhile, notions about both matter and machines have changed so greatly since 1900 that it may be more accurate to call the intellectually dominant view today materialistic reductionism, dropping the term *mechanism*. At the same time various forms of dualism, pluralism, and pan-psychism remain alive in contemporary thought, as does a widespread belief in survival, as we saw in Chapter One. All this suggests that one should not rule out *a priori* any of the major contending ontologies. Thus we shall hold the ontological question in suspense until Part Four.

3

What Justifies Belief?

What kind of evidence would give rational warrant for believing in survival after death? We here cannot expect to gain certainty about it. Survival is not logically or analytically certain. Nor can it be proved with the practical certainty that experimental testing provides for various hypotheses in natural science. However, we shall take a scientific approach in our inquiry. This will be the kind of approach used on complex questions by investigators in the social and behavioral sciences, and used often in practical life as well. This approach can yield a confirmed plausible basis for belief, and that is what we seek. The approach has three stages. Taken together, they form a kind of obstacle course, a long course but a rewarding one. The three stages, as applied to our inquiry are:

First, the hypothesis must have initial plausibility. That is, it must not be founded on a logical, linguistic, or similar mistake. Some philosophers have claimed that the survival idea is based on just that sort of mistake. We shall consider those claims in Chapter Four.

Second, the hypothesis must fit plausibly with the relevant factual evidence. Most of our inquiry will be devoted to this stage. The key factual issue for us is whether the organic part of the human self, which perishes at death, is distinct and separable from the meaningful core of the self, which might survive. We shall investigate this first by looking at memory. Individual memories are crucial to one's personal identity. If they are all lodged in the brain, personal survival becomes dubious; but the evidence may lead us in a different direction.

We shall then seek a plausible view of the self's structure and dynamics. Such a view could provide for a distinct inmost self not reducible to the brain. We inquire also whether the self is inextricably dependent on social structures, as claimed by some. We then explore further the inmost self, asking whether any kinds of mental activities occur in it that might survive the organism's death. We scrutinize also the perceptual process. We conclude that a wide variety of evidence about the human self can fit plausibly with our survival hypothesis. Moreover, since this evidence is interconnected, the variety of favorable results strengthens the credibility of survival.

Third, the hypothesis being tested should cohere comfortably with overall human knowledge. In our inquiry, this means the survival hypothesis should cohere with a defensible ontology, that is, with a defensible view of the overall structure of reality. This question is examined in Part Four. There we note that survival does fit with some twentieth-century philosophies of becoming, which emphasize the key role of existential time. In Part Four we also explore what kind of survival may be plausible, the evidence from extrasensory experience, and various wider questions about a universe in which survival is not a peculiar oddity but a coherent part of the whole. Finally, we reach a comprehensive judgment as to the confirmed plausibility of personal survival after death.

Before turning now to the inquiry itself, I want to comment on the use of plausibility as a criterion for judgment. This term is rather widely employed by philosophers and scientists, usually without a clear definition. I have elsewhere developed a nine-point scale for ranking confirmed plausibility.[1] Here, however, I expect we shall use only two of these rankings, with their correlative opposites for implausibility: *High* plausibility means a claim is supported by a preponderance of evidence that is clear, strong, and convincing. *Moderate* plausibility means a claim is supported by substantial evidence that outweighs the opposing evidence. These ratings are based largely on criteria used by courts.[2] Since we are dealing here not with certain knowledge but with an effort to reach sound opinions, it seems reasonable to draw on the institution with most practical experience in such efforts, that is, the judicial system. (I also use a ranking of *maximal* plausibility, signifying a claim credible beyond any reasonable doubt; but I do not expect to find such cases in our present inquiry.)

II

Objections and Refutations

4

Approach through Analysis

Various philosophers have held that the survival hypothesis cannot be made plausible because it is based on a mistake. Such an error is said to rule out plausible survival analytically, without going through any long collection and sifting of factual evidence. If this be true, then we should wind up our inquiry right now, for the survival hypothesis will have lost its needed initial plausibility. But how weighty are these analytic objections? Let us have a brief look at the major ones. I shall quote these from various recent philosophers and from one famous eighteenth-century thinker, David Hume.

1. *Personal survival cannot be rationally argued because personal identity is a fiction.* This view was espoused by Hume in some striking passages of his *Treatise:*

> For my part, when I enter most intimately into what I call *myself,* I always stumble on some particular perception or other, of heat or cold, light or shade, love or hatred, pain or pleasure. I never can catch *myself* at any time without a perception, and never can observe anything but the perception. When my perceptions are remov'd for any time, as by sound sleep; so long am I insensible of *myself,* and may truly be said not to exist. And were all my perceptions remov'd by death, and cou'd I neither think, nor feel, nor see, nor love, nor hate after the dissolution of my body, I shou'd be entirely

annihilated, nor do I conceive what is farther requisite to make me a perfect non-entity.[1]

We are, adds Hume, "nothing but a bundle or collection of different perceptions," and "the identity, which we ascribe to the mind of man, is only a fictitious one . . . "

Hume himself, however, soon found serious flaws in this theory of mind. Indeed he omitted this moment-to-moment theory of personal identity in later writings, including his critical essay "On the Immortality of the Soul." If continuing personal identity is a fiction, how do I integrate and retain any knowledge over time? Moreover, if I no longer exist when sleeping, by what miracle do I awaken with all the memories, habits, skills, and projects that I had before I slept? These objections make Hume's moment-to-moment view of the person highly implausible. On the positive side, we shall seek a plausible view of the self later in Part Two.

2. *Survival is meaningless because death ends the world.* This view comes from Ludwig Wittgenstein, who wrote in his *Tractatus* that "at death the world does not alter but comes to an end." By this he seems to mean that we can logically know, and speak about, only the world of experienceable facts—and "we do not live to experience death." Whatever might lie "beyond death" is a riddle, a mystical question that cannot even be put into words.[2]

The same point has been advanced by other philosophers in the Wittgenstein tradition. Logical positivists developed further this approach, with their criterion of verifiability.[3] Earlier, Hume had voiced a similar view, near the end of his immortality essay: "By what argument or analogies can we prove any state of existence, which no one ever saw, and which no way resembles any that ever was seen? . . . Some new species of logic is requisite for that purpose, and some new faculties of mind, that they may enable us to comprehend that logic."[4]

However, the claim that we cannot speak meaningfully about unexperienceable states of affairs is contrary to fact. Electrons and other elementary particles are completely unexperienceable by humans, and so are—at the other end of the scale—distant galaxies detected by radio-telescopes. Meaningful theories are constructed about these transcendent entities, and plausible beliefs are developed. Such theories and beliefs make use of analogy. Metaphors and models, including mathematical equations, are used to bring these into human thought and communication. Similar procedures can be used in dealing with survival of death.[5]

At a more human level, no serious investigator doubts today that much of our mind's activity goes on unconsciously. This too, like death, is beyond our experience; but we can deduce it, and we experience its effects. This area of mental activity will be explored at length in Part Three.

Positivists will object that scientific entities, as well as unconscious mental events, create effects or leave traces that are detectible and experienceable. These, they say, give factual ground for investigation and belief. But the same appears to hold true for survival. Even though we the living cannot experience a postmortem existence, many personal reports do exist claiming to describe some experience of survival. These cannot reasonably be rejected out of hand on logical grounds. We need no new logic here, as Hume claimed, but rather an openness to inquiry.

3. *To speak of surviving death makes no linguistic sense.* The British philosopher D. Z. Phillips, for example, declares: "If one understands what is meant by 'survival' and what is meant by 'death,' then one is at a loss to know what it means to talk of surviving death." The question cannot be considered a factual one, he claims, for "here we do not really know what is being asked." Nor is the problem due to inadequacies of language. Our language is the only means of communication and it makes no sense, he says, to suppose that language itself is inadequate. While Phillips can find no way to say what survival might be like, he goes on to say what it *can't* be like, namely, human life as we know it.[6]

Antony Flew expresses similar but more limited objections. "The difficulty," he says, "is to change the use of person words so radically that it becomes significant to talk of people surviving dissolution: without changing it to such an extent that these vital logical liaisons (in present usage) are lost."[7]

Here I am tempted to offer some joking advice to these philosophers: they should read a bit of science fiction. Our language does seem adequate to convey the notion of person-like beings elsewhere in space, though their physical attributes may differ notably from ours. Likewise our language can draw an imaginative picture of person-like survival after death, as many people have found. The key questions are: *Could such survival include continuing existence for one's essential self, and does it plausibly do so?* This requires deciding a number of questions, including the nature of the self. But these all involve empirical issues and are not to be legislated on linguistic grounds. We shall examine these questions in due course.

4. *To assert personal survival mistakes the nature of man.* This objection is probably held more deeply, and argued more forcefully, than any other. Gilbert Ryle claims it is a "category mistake" to suppose an inner separable mind in our organic body, a "ghost in the machine." Rather, "when we describe people as exercising qualities of mind, we are not referring to occult episodes of which their overt acts and utterances are effects; we are referring to those overt acts and utterances themselves." Thus for Ryle a person largely *is* what he does in the world. This clearly rules out survival, though Ryle doesn't argue that point.[8]

Other philosophers admit that inner activities occur but insist that our inner life is united with our body and with our social environment, thus making survival incredible. Phillips writes that "unless there were a common life which people share, which they were taught and came to learn, there could be no notion of a person." This being so, he argues, what it means to be a person "cannot be divorced or abstracted" from these common features of human life. The idea of personal survival apart from these external features is thus, he claims, "fundamentally confused."[9]

This is a key theme also for Corliss Lamont in his treatise against immortality. In addition, he writes, "to the indissoluble union between body, on the one hand, and mind and personality, on the other, there is also an indissoluble connection between the body-mind-personality, that is, the whole man, and the sustaining and conditioning environment, both human and physical.'' The mind/body issue, Lamont argues, holds the key to possible survival of death, and this issue has in effect been settled since ''the monistic relationship between personality or mind and body is an established psychological law.'' Thus, for Lamont, survival is impossible.[10]

A number of other philosophers have expounded an identity theory of mind/brain relations. This form of monistic reductionism would rule out survival, except by a miracle.

However, although the monistic view of man is sometimes phrased analytically—or even held as an unquestioned postulate—its truth depends crucially upon empirical facts, as the above philosophers would doubtless agree. What is the real nature of man? Is the whole of our personality or self contained in our organism? Is it completely dependent on our organism? Admitting that each of us is very much shaped by social influences, is it certain that nothing personal could exist beyond the grave? We shall address these factual questions later in this inquiry.

Thus we find no warrant for any of the main claims that personal survival must be ruled out from the start as a ''mistake.'' Each of these claims is based not only on principles but on certain beliefs about the facts. Those beliefs as to the facts are subject to challenge and investigation; this we shall give them as we proceed, turning now to the empirical part of our inquiry.

5

Approach through Memory

The sharpest empirical attack on personal survival centers on the status of memory. Bertrand Russell, for example, argues that our personal identity amounts to nothing more than a series of experiences, connected by memory and habits. Our memories and habits, he suggests, are bound up with the structure of the brain as a river is connected with the river bed. The water in the river is always changing, but its course stays the same because previous rains have worn a channel. So, too, previous events have worn a channel in the brain, and our thoughts flow along this channel. This, says Russell, is the cause of memory and mental habits. "But the brain, as a structure," he declares, "is dissolved at death, and memory therefore may be expected to be also dissolved." Thus the person that I am must also dissolve at death.[1]

Lamont is even more forceful on this theme. A "worthwhile personal immortality," he writes, depends "above all on memory, in order that there shall be in the hereafter a sense of identity and the ability to recognize self as well as others." For memory, he notes, is basic "to the sense of personal identity we have in life." However, the proper functioning of memory "clearly depends in the first place on the associational patterns laid down as enduring structural imprints" in the brain. "But these pathways, these memory patterns, these records—millions and billions of them—are all imbedded in the gray cortical matter of the brain." Thus when the brain dissolves, Lamont argues, our memory also must vanish.[2]

Both of these writers are here making three distinct points: (1) Memories are necessary to personal identity and the self. (2) Memories are preserved only in the brain. (3) Therefore, when the brain perishes at death, memories must go with it; this entails disappearance of personal identity and along with it any hope of personal survival.

This appears to be a valid argument, in the sense that if the two premises are true, the conclusion follows. Some theologians, while admitting the premises, have attempted to deny the full conclusion. They accept that the brain, the body, and personal identity do perish at death, but they affirm that God has power to resurrect what has perished utterly, and God will do so.[3] This anticipates a greater shift from the usual course of nature than in the traditional Christian view. The latter posits an immortal soul continuing after death of the human organism and available for personal resurrection.[4] The present inquiry, however, will not seek to refute the Russell-Lamont argument by asserting any kind of theological views. Rather, it appears that *the first premise advanced by Russell-Lamont is true, but the second one is false, and thus the conclusion does not follow.*

As to the first premise, many philosophers have noted the key link between memories and our sense of personal identity. None, as far as I know, has disputed this. The enduring contents that lie behind our feeling of personal identity appear, quite clearly, to consist of memories. No one else has *my* memories. These are strung out over a long series of years, all of which were *my* years, as remembered. How thronging these memories are, if one lets them emerge. And how many more lie concealed behind the veil. These memories establish my own sense of continuing identity. The belief that I am, in large part, the same person I was five years ago depends on the further belief that I-now and I-then both share the same memories of earlier years. The other more tangible entities that add to my sense of present reality—my own organism, my possessions, my interactions with people close to me—all take on meaning because of what *has been* between us, because of the ties built up: and I am aware of this through memory.

However, personal identity is not simply a vast array of memories, inert and changeless. An active principle seems also to be at work in us, a principle that *uses* memories. This principle, too, appears crucial to continuing personal identity, and we shall later investigate it.

Our present effort will be to examine the second premise of the Russell-Lamont argument, namely, that memories are preserved only in the brain. To do this fruitfully, we need first to be clear about the nature of memory and the nature of the brain. Both of these are highly complex, incompletely known, and the subjects of widespread and intensive inquiries. All we can hope to do is to get conceptually clear about them.

Memory is more than one thing. We first distinguish very short-term memories, which may possibly be linked to reverberating circuits in the brain, from long-term memories. We here are concerned only with the latter. With them, one can distinguish three kinds of memory operations: *recalling,* or retrieving, which depends on prior *storing,* which depends on prior *acquiring.* Our present interest focuses on memory storage. Here, the storing of habit memories, that is, our learned action patterns, may well consist primarily of response systems in the brain. But our sense of personal identity emerges rather from the store of pure memories. By *pure memories,* following the philosopher Henri Bergson, is meant our remembering of past individual episodes (as imagery) and of past insights and conceivings (as propositions and concepts).[5] *Does the brain plausibly hold the store of pure memories?* Before examining the evidence on that, let us take a look at the brain itself.

6

The Human Brain

The human brain is the most complex and extraordinary of all biological structures. It forms the operating core of our central nervous system. Our brain receives information messages via nerve pathways from our sense receptors, sends out motoric action messages to muscles, interacts with the autonomic nervous system, and serves as the biological substrate for some if not all of our mental life.[1] To find whether part of our mental life and our memory store are separable from the brain—as we seek to do—we must first look at the brain itself. This will be a careful look, but a general one. I shall limit the account to what is needed for our inquiry.

Physically, the average human brain weighs about 1,400 grams. The size can vary greatly, however. Ivan Turgenev reportedly had a brain over twice the size of Anatole France's, yet both were highly intelligent. Physiologists estimate our brain holds some ten to twelve billion neurons or nerve cells.[2] In addition to these neurons, the brain contains about ten times as many other cells, called glial cells, which occupy about forty per cent of the space; these support and separate the neurons physically and are not very active electrically.

Neurons have the unique property of efficiently transmitting electrical energy along their length. Then, by jumping the synaptic gap between two neurons, using chemicals called neurotransmitters, the electric charge sweeps quickly forward to another neuron. This is the primary message system in the brain and central nervous system.

A neuron consists of a cell body, an axon or transmitting fiber, and a set of dendrites or receptor fibers. Both axon and dendrites emerge from the central cell body. One authority reports that everyday a large mammalian neuron has to synthesize from nutrients about a third of the protein in its cell body.[3] More broadly, the proteins and other large molecules (macromolecular components) in our brain neurons are renewed about ten thousand times in a normal lifetime.[4] These are key facts to note in considering brain storage of memories.

Human neurons, unlike other cells, do not divide and reproduce themselves; nor can brain neurons repair themselves if injured. Thus the young person has as many neurons as the older one. In fact, he or she has more, since brain neurons die at a noticeable rate. However, there is an increase with age in "neuronal arborization," that is, multiplication of dendrites or receptor fibers. Also, repeated use of certain synapses between neurons may make them more efficient in transmitting. This may offer a neurological clue to repetitive learning and habit memory.

Most neuronal functioning in the brain is believed to take place not as single-link chains of neurons but as what neurophysiologist Sir John Eccles calls "wave fronts."[5] This enables far greater accuracy and flexibility of transmission. One must not, however, view the brain as simply a diffuse mass of shifting neuronal networks. A good deal of localization of brain function has been mapped over the past fifty years, much of it by a remarkable brain surgeon, Wilder Penfield, and his colleagues at Montreal Neurological Institute.

Three, sometimes four, sections of the brain are distinguished. In an evolutionary sense, all of these are outgrowths of the spinal cord. They are the hindbrain, the midbrain, and finally the forebrain, consisting of two general areas, the diencephalon and telencephalon. The diencephalon, more or less in the center of the head, includes the thalamus and several other segments. The telencephalon includes what most of us think of as the *real* human brain, the two cerebral hemispheres and their thin crumpled outer gray layer of cortex. The cerebral cortex, in fact, contains three quarters of all neurons in the brain. Neurologically speaking, it is what makes us human. As shown by the diagram, various lobes have been labeled in the cerebral hemispheres. Also, as indicated, various speech and functional areas have been identified in the cerebral cortex. These are important to our later discussions.

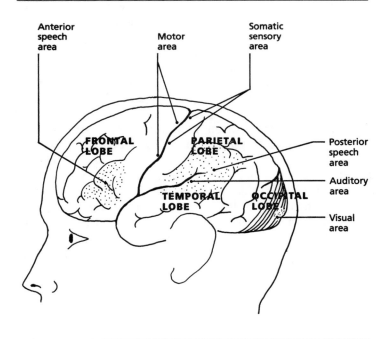

Figure 1. *Simplified Left Cerebral Cortex*

Several other points should be noted about the cerebral hemispheres. First, of course, there are two of them, right and left. The connections between them and the two sides of the body are interesting. The right half of our visual field, from both eyes, is represented in the primary visual center of the left occipital cortex, and vice versa. The auditory pathways, in contrast, go from each inner ear to both sides of the brain. The somatic-sensory pathways and the motor pathways cross over from the cortex to the opposite side of the body. The speech areas build up in one dominant hemisphere, usually the left. Interrelations between hemispheres are handled by several connections. Much publicity has been given to "split brain" patients;[6] some overly sweeping conclusions have been drawn from these, but the valid results seem consonant with the approach taken in our inquiry.

Second, all the incoming sensory impulses except smell pass through the centrally placed thalamus on their way to the cortex. Indeed, the thalamus—in conjunction with the small hypothalamus and some other central brain areas—seems to play a key role as a kind of relay station and primary integrating system.[7]

Third, two other important nonspecific brain systems have been distinguished by physiologists. The reticular activating, or arousal, system is involved with alertness, attention, arousal, and sleep. The limbic system plays an important but ill-defined role in regulating emotion.

Fourth, neurons of the sensory cortex are reportedly arranged in highly stratified fashion into vertical columns or "modules." This arrangement may occur in other parts of the cortex also.[8] We shall see later how these aspects of brain function relate to our inquiry into survival.

7

Evidence on Memory–I

Having analyzed various aspects of memory and the brain, let us now examine some evidence about where "pure" memories of individual experiences and insights are stored. These are the memories that establish our personal identity, and if they are most plausibly stored in the brain, then the Russell-Lamont argument will have won. In that case, personal survival after death could only occur through supernatural intervention. But if the pure memory store is not plausibly located in the brain, then the issue remains open at the naturalistic level, and we shall have to rethink the question of how such memories might be stored. For the moment we need chiefly to keep our minds flexible. We need to refrain from imposing on the evidence any preformed theory—for example, the theory that memories *must* be stored in the brain or in some other physical system. Let us, rather, open ourselves to the evidence about memory storage, taken from neurology, neurophysiology, psychology, psychiatry, and phenomenology. We begin with some remarkable neurological findings.

Imagine yourself in the operating room of a Montreal hospital. The patient on the operating table is fully conscious, even though he is undergoing a brain operation. He is a twenty-five-year-old French Canadian, Sylvere B., who began having epileptic seizures six years ago. In his early attacks he would hear someone calling his name, "Sylvere, Sylvere, Sylvere . . . " This and other symptoms indicated that he might be suffering from abnormality in one focal point of the brain. Dr. Wilder Penfield, a noted brain surgeon and neurologist, decided to operate on Sylvere B., hoping to locate and cut out this focal lesion without injury to any mental function. This is an operation Penfield pioneered several decades ago.[1]

To guard against cutting out vital brain tissue, Penfield devised an elaborate mapping system. Using mild electrical stimulation, he probed different points in the patient's cortex while it was opened up in the operating room and observed the patient's reaction. Thus he developed a functional map of that particular patient's brain before he did any cutting. And, by accumulating hundreds of these maps, Penfield and his colleagues (as stated earlier) were able to draw a functional diagram for much of the cortex in the normal or average human brain. Drugs and other procedures are now generally used instead of this technique in severe epilepsy, but Penfield's findings remain fundamental to our knowledge of the brain.

For us the key point is what Penfield found about the store of pure memories. With Sylvere, and with various other patients, Penfield evoked "experiential" responses by stimulating points on the temporal cortex. Thus, when the electrode touched point 16 with Sylvere, the patient said: "Something brings back a memory, I could see Seven-Up Bottling Company—Harrison Bakery." Stimulating another point evoked a conversation, "just like a dream." Another evoked the sound of a theme song from a radio program, which Sylvere proceeded to sing. Likewise with other patients: A woman heard a choir singing "White Christmas." A woman saw herself meet a friend on the street, and at another point she heard her mother "yelling at my little sister, Mary Jane." Another young woman found herself in a familiar office with desks, "and someone was calling to me, a man leaning on a desk with a pencil in his hand." A man from South Africa, stimulated at point 7, exclaimed in surprise: "Yes, Doctor, yes, Doctor! Now I hear people laughing—my friends in South Africa," specifically two girl cousins. Forty patients altogether reported such experiences, based on operating room records, out of some eleven hundred who were tested during epilepsy surgery. Summarizing this evidence, Penfield has written:

> When stimulation has produced an experiential response during operative exploration, the patient has usually recognized that this was something out of his own past. At the same time he may have been acutely aware of the fact that he was lying upon the operating table. Thus, he was able to contemplate and to talk about this doubling of awareness and to recognize it as a strange paradox . . . .
>
> Some patients call an experiential response a dream. Others state that it is a 'flashback' from their own life history. All agree that it is more vivid than anything they could recollect voluntarily . . . . When, by chance, the neurosurgeon's electrode activates past experience, that experience unfolds progressively, moment by moment . . . . There is no holding it still, no turning back, no crossing with other periods. When the electrode is withdrawn, it stops as suddenly as it began. A particular strip can sometimes be repeated by interrupting the stimulation and then shortly reapplying it at the same or a nearby point. In that case it begins at the same moment of time on each occasion.[2]

Truly these findings are extraordinary. They strongly suggest that people retain pure memories in far more detail than they are aware of, and that these include rather small experiences, not only the crucial moments in their lives. However, the memories evoked by Penfield probably related to events that were attentively noticed when they first happened. For the persons involved, they were not wholly trivial or unremarked experiences.

Some commentators have played down the significance of Penfield's findings about memory. This is partly because Penfield claimed he was evoking an actual record of past experience. Many of us at times reshape our memories, as recalled, to fit our present life needs. Thus what we think we remember is inaccurate. However, it seems unlikely that Penfield's patients were either reshaping their memories or fantasizing or prevaricating. They were surprised and often astonished at their experiential responses, which came in the midst of numerous other kinds of response to the widespread electrode probings. They had every motive to tell the truth, since the surgeon was relying on their reports to know where to cut in their brains. Moreover, Penfield often checked later with the patients as to whether the experiential responses derived from real past events, and in some cases (e.g., the songs) the responses clearly must have represented a memory. Thus it seems highly plausible, as Penfield affirms, that most of these responses were "reproductions of past experience."

Is the record of that past experience—the store of our pure memories—lodged in the temporal cortex touched by Penfield's electrodes? Not according to Penfield. "Since excision of these areas does not abolish memory," he observed, "they do not contain the actual record of the past." A similar conclusion derives, by analogy, from the fact that in other cortical areas "the effect of electrical stimulation is to interfere with cortical function," not to arouse it.[3] What role, then, does this area of temporal cortex play in our lives? Penfield calls this the "interpretive" cortex. Building on his ideas, here is how it may work:

Memory normally serves us here in answering the primal questions about any object or situation we encounter, namely: what is it, and is it good or bad for me? As Penfield notes, this requires a scanning process or, more broadly, a system of "recall and comparison and interpretation." In daily life practically all of that occurs subconsciously; only the conclusions come into awareness. If this were not so—if we were often subject to the double consciousness reported by Penfield's patients—no doubt we should become, as he suggests, "hopelessly confused."[4] But thanks to inhibitive control by the "interpretive" cortex, perhaps as part of a wider system, our pure memories are almost always fleeting and shadowy, if they reach consciousness at all. This view accords with Penfield's discovery that his electrical stimulation in other areas usually blocked normal functioning. So too, in the "interpretive" cortex, the electrode blocked normal inhibition and allowed a replay of a segment of pure memory, in those patients whose inhibitory system was already worn down by past epileptic discharges.

Let us be clear what we are saying here. Temporal cortex plays a role in recall of pure memories and in inhibiting such recall. It does not hold the store of our pure memories. And that is the question before us: *Are pure memories stored in the brain?*

Penfield, along with most brain scientists, assumed that memories must be stored in the brain. Since they are not held in the temporal lobes, he proposed that the memory store might be in the hippocampal areas in the central part of the brain and "their integrating circuits."[5] Later he shifted to a more vague statement: "The record may be located in the diencephalon," that is, the thalamus and surrounding central areas.[6] But one of Penfield's colleagues, H. H. Jasper, pointed out in the same colloquium that lesions affecting "the hippocampal system bilaterally and related portions of the brain stem and mesial thalamus in man may prevent the storage of long-term memories" but "this does not imply a localization of memory traces in these structures, since recall of already established memories is preserved."[7] A similar point is made by Jacques Barbizet, a French neurologist specializing in memory problems. He writes that "these lesions do not seem to destroy earlier information that the patient recognizes and that can be extracted from him, fragment by fragment . . . . "[8] Thus these drastic injuries to the central part of the brain (bilateral destruction of the hippocampus and widespread other bilateral injury) destroy a person's ability to remember new events, but not his memory store.

Despite this, one might ask: Isn't it possible that one of the small parts of the central brain—so far unmentioned—might serve as the memory warehouse? That, however, seems to be ruled out by the great number and variety of our pure memories and the very much greater complexity required in any neuronal memory store that would hold and retrieve these memories. As neuropsychologist Karl Lashley pointed out many years ago, this "precludes any concept of a center of consciousness as a limited center where information is accumulated, for the complexity of mental processes is far too great to be represented by the permutations of a small number of cells. Such a center might act as a pacemaker but not as an organizer or terminal receiver."[9]

This brings us to the other leading candidate as a memory storehouse in the brain—the frontal lobes. Here Barbizet reports that total destruction of the two frontal lobes brings about such apathy and such a reduction in language that no study of memory is possible. However, smaller injuries to the frontal lobes hurt the patient's ability to plan and choose rather than destroying memories.[10] Various cases have been studied. For example, a middle-aged stockbroker had half or more of both frontal lobes removed as radical treatment for a large tumor. He was studied extensively for five years thereafter. Neurologist D. Denny-Brown, reporting on the case, states: "There was no defect in response to tests for aphasia [language memory loss], but occasional minor dysphasia was noted in prolonged conversation."[11]

Another patient who was carefully studied by Penfield's former colleague, psychologist Donald Hebb, had both prefrontal lobes removed, losing about 15 percent of the total weight of his cerebrum. "No clinical or psychometric deterioration could be detected," Penfield notes. "Although he may have lacked initiative, he managed to find and to hold employment and satisfy his family."[12] Even more striking is a further case reported by Hebb. There, after removal of his left prefrontal lobe, a young man proceeded to make a perfect Stanford-Binet I.Q. score, and comparable scores on all the other intelligence tests, verbal or nonverbal, that Hebb could give him. Hebb writes: "Not one person in a thousand—or ten thousand—could have done as well, brain operation or no."[13] Such an intelligence score would, of course, require a fully functioning memory.

A further reason for doubting that the frontal lobes store our pure memories lies in the results of prefrontal lobotomies performed on many mental patients. This operation slices through the connections between a major part of the frontal lobes and the rest of the brain. Whatever other damaging effects these procedures may have, they do not usually seem to destroy the memory store. According to Denny-Brown, "As the first results of the operation pass off . . . general memory rapidly returns."[14]

More broadly, both human and animal brains have been subjected to drastic overall changes of state without destroying long-term memories. These "insults" include the electrical storms of epilepsy and of electroshock treatment, and periods of deep coma, anesthesia, or extreme cooling, suffered naturally by ill humans or imposed experimentally on animals.[15] It seems possible that habit memory—that is, repetitively learned skill responses—might be represented in the brain by a pattern of very stable synaptic or other neuronal changes that would survive these massive insults. But pure memory—that is, retention of a single experienced event or cognized proposition—could hardly be registered so deeply in any set of neurons that it would survive massive electrical discharges, "freezing," or some of the other insults.

Ralph W. Gerard, a neurophysiologist, summed it up as early as 1953, writing that memory

> . . . localization largely vanishes when we look at the effects of brain damage. Large sections of nearly any part of the brain can be destroyed without loss of particular memories or, indeed, without disturbance of the memory function. Human brains have been extensively damaged by trauma, by tumors or abscesses, by loss of circulation, by operative removal, or by the shriveling away of extreme age. In these cases the ability to learn new things, to make sound judgments, to see new relations and to imagine new ideas may be profoundly disturbed, but the recollection of past experience is likely to remain reasonably intact.[16]

From this analysis, what shall we conclude? Earlier we assigned a high plausibility to Penfield's view that the pure memory record is not in the temporal cortex and that the relevant temporal areas do play a role in regulating memory recall. However, the further claim that the brain somewhere holds the record of past experience appears, on the present evidence, to be highly implausible, as applied to pure memories. This gravely undercuts the Russell-Lamont thesis that the memory store is deposited in the brain—thus undercutting their argument against personal identity after death.

But we need a wider perspective. In the next chapter we shall see what the neurophysiologists, psychologists, and psychiatrists have to add to our inquiry.

8

Evidence on Memory–II

Neurophysiologists experimenting with animals, often using electrodes implanted in the brain, have developed several different theories about how memory works. Their ideas fall into two general groups, neuronal theories and nonspecific theories. The neuronal advocates think that the key to memory storage involves long-term changes in synaptic junctions, in neuron-glial relations, in chemical balance within the neuron, or even in the chemicals (nucleotide bases) within each neuron's macromolecules. The nonspecific theorists stress mass action, systems concepts, or temporal statistical patterns. Each of these approaches has grave problems. The nonspecific theories focus on what appears to happen in the brain during recall. They seem to have no real explanation for memory *storage*. The neuronal theorists have explanations for storage, but their theories don't seem to fit the facts.[1]

On this latter point an important critical review has been written by E. Roy John, director of the Brain Research Laboratories at New York Medical College (New York University). John first published this review in 1972; he reaffirmed it, with further strengthening evidence, in 1980.[2] John considers the research evidence bearing on the theory that experiences make a "groove" of increased excitability along specific neural paths and that this groove is the stored memory. We have heard this notion already from Russell and Lamont. It is a common element in neuronal theories of memory storage.

However, John reports that "countless experiments" with animals, destroying or removing parts of their brains, have "failed to locate the site of the connection of any pathway responsible for memory." Moreover, he cites various facts that make the theory implausible. Thus, he reports, brain neurons often fire spontaneously. They respond in a variable way to any given stimulus. They respond in the same way to stimuli coming from different sense organs. In view of this, he suggests, the brain cannot assign any specific significance to a discharge by a specific neuron in a particular pathway.

Clearly, as John points out, cellular changes do take place in learning. But the problem for the neuronal memory theorist is that these cellular changes are far too widespread for his theory to deal with. John cites numerous examples indicating that the process of learning influences great numbers of neurons in many brain regions, even with the simple tasks studied by animal researchers. When every new experience affects so many neurons, he points out, it is hard to imagine how any pathway could be protected from constant alterations, which would destroy its presumed memory function. John seems fully justified when he concludes: "It is highly unlikely that memory consists of the establishment or facilitation of a specific neural pathway in which firing constitutes remembering."

Based on the evidence about human brains from Penfield and others, and now on the neurophysiological results from animal experiments, we are close to confirming the implausibility of the Russell-Lamont claim that pure memories are stored in the brain. That is, this hypothesis seems opposed by a preponderance of evidence that is clear, strong, and convincing, making the claim highly implausible. The brain evidently is involved in acquiring pure memories, but it seems not to be a place where they are stored. We still have some distance to go, however, on the issue of memory storage.

* * *

We shift now to a further key question on memory: *Do people in fact retain true memories of their past?* Some psychologists claim that recall is often, if not always, a "reconstructive" process. Does this mean that one's true past has utterly vanished, that what one takes to be true memories are nothing more than a present experience built up from ambiguous traces left behind by a past now dead and gone? If so, then personal identity, and human existence, shrink to a present reality only. In that case, since one's present reality is closely linked to one's organism, the chances for survival after death seem meager. We shall explore this question—the question of the veracity of pure memories—through the findings of some psychologists and psychiatrists.

How many pure memories do people actually retain? The answer is hard to uncover. Very often we remember wrongly. Our recall of a past experience gets truncated, telescoped, twisted, reinterpreted, run in with another, screened, or wholly blocked. Such results may be influenced by our current feelings and mind-set. Various studies have documented these facts, and ordinary experience confirms them.[3] On the other hand, most of us are quite sure we can remember accurately many facts out of our past. At times we have occasion to check these and find we were correct. More difficult are the cases when we recall not merely facts but a particular episode in some detail, and we feel sure it did happen thus. But how can we test this?

Some psychologists, working with hypnotic age-regression, have developed strong indications of a hidden pure memory store. In hypnotic age-regression a subject is hypnotized, told to regress himself or herself to an earlier age, and then asked to respond to questions. In one experiment Margaret Brenman at the Menninger Clinic asked her subjects to recall fairy tales they had heard in childhood and not reread since. These recollections were compared with published versions of the originals. They showed major omissions and distortions. Brenman then hypnotized the subjects and again asked them to reproduce the same story, with much improved results. Thematic Apperception Tests (T.A.T.) were also given. Comparing the normal and hypnotic reproductions with each other and with the results of the T.A.T., Brenman found that the omissions and distortions in the normal reproduction correspond to present "emotional needs" of the subjects.[4] So here we have a clear case where pure memories were retained from childhood (since they could be evoked under hypnosis), but selective blocking and distortion of these memories took place as a present process, responding to current emotional needs.

Another case in which a man overcame a severe emotional blockage was recounted by a prison psychologist. A prisoner had run away from home at an early age, hating his father. The father later deserted the mother, and when he died left a sizable estate. The prisoner wanted his mother to get this money, but he could not remember anything about his mother except that she was always crying. He couldn't recall the name of the town or even the state where they lived. Not even under hypnosis did these names emerge. All he recalled was once taking a train ride.

The psychologist suggested to the hypnotized prisoner that he would remember the train conductor calling out the name of the approaching town. This brought forth, finally, a town's name, and also the surname of a family living in that town. The psychologist then contacted all six towns of that name in the United States and eventually traced the prisoner's mother.[5] Here two small boyhood facts—a conductor's call and the name of a neighbor family—were finally and accurately evoked, many years later, despite the prisoner's continuing emotional blockages.

Another intriguing experiment was carried out by Robert True at the University of Vermont School of Medicine. True reflected that for young children their birthday is a major event. They look forward to the party, ask their mothers when it's coming, and no doubt focus on the idea that it will happen "next Tuesday" (or whatever other day). But after the birthday is over, the fact of its having been on a Tuesday loses all importance, and this surely is the kind of memory one would expect to vanish from any neuronal memory bank. Also, however, this is a fact that can be accurately checked. If Subject A, an adult, has his birthday on June 23 and if he was seven years old in 1960, the experimenter can simply look in a 200-year calendar and find the day of the week of A's seventh birthday. If A imagines now that it was Tuesday, or guesses at it, his chance of guessing right would be one-seventh or about 14 percent. Moreover, True noted, the same considerations apply to Christmas during childhood.

True put a total of fifty subjects (forty men and ten women, aged twenty to twenty-four) under deep hypnosis and regressed each of them to their tenth birthday and their tenth Christmas. At that age, 92 percent named the correct day of the week for their birthday and 94 percent for Christmas. When regressed to age seven, 84 percent named the correct day of the week for their birthday and 86 percent for Christmas. When regressed to age four, 62 percent named the correct day for their birthday and 76 percent for Christmas. Apparently the great majority of these fifty people did have buried memories of the day of the week of their birthdays and Christmases. Of course, as True pointed out, he was dealing with a selected group, all of whom had previously been regressed to at least the age of five. All were excellent hypnotic subjects, chosen from a larger group of 175.[6]

True's findings have been attacked because he had a 200-year calendar with him at the time of the age regressions. He thus knew the right answers and might have unknowingly communicated those answers to some of his subjects. However, some others seeking to replicate True's experiment got less striking results, though better than chance. Ernest Hilgard, a psychologist at Stanford, with between twenty-eight and thirty-two subjects, found that 55 percent could be regressed to an early birthday and 79 percent to an early Christmas.[7] We may conclude that many, though probably not all, of these early day-of-the-week responses were genuine buried memories. It seems highly implausible that such memories could be stored so many years in a person's brain, with no repetitive activity to establish them as a habit, with no reinforcement after the one holiday passed so long ago, and with the brain's neurological structure subject to incessant activity, day and night, throughout the whole period.

Coming back to the question of how pure memories become distorted as a present process, the English psychologist Ian Hunter has offered a personal example. He reports at age twenty-seven seeing again a school which he had visited just once before when he was four years old. Earlier on several occasions he had vividly recalled the school's large playground, its enormous gymnasium, and the whole building's vast proportions. Twenty-three years later he was struck with how alarmingly the school had shrunk, how tiny its playground and classrooms now were, compared with his memory of them. Yet he was assured by others that this in fact was the same school.[8]

Now this is a kind of experience many of us have. What happened to change Hunter's early memory of the school was clearly a present process. But consider also the further implications. The colors, physical layout, and feelings-of-relative-size of this school had remained in Hunter's pure memory store from the age of four onward, based only on a single visit plus several later recollections. A brain-storage theory of memory would have to posit that some chemical or electrical patterning of neurons was laid down in Hunter's brain at the age of four, from that single visit, and this remained so little changed twenty-three years later that the four-year-old's feelings-of-relative-size would still be vividly evoked, confronting and confusing the adult's new feelings-of-size on seeing the school again. Here again, from what we know of brain functioning, this assumption seems highly implausible.

Here is one further small experiment on the evoking of old memories. Psychologist Silvan Tomkins asked each subject to shout, before a group, at the top of his or her voice, the words, "No, I won't!" Some subjects refused. Most reluctantly agreed to do it. The consequences of this performance, Tomkins reported, are varied. Most adults protruded their lower lip immediately after speaking. Many said they re-experienced childish feelings of distress and anger, with recall of "long forgotten specific incidents in which such defeat was evoked."[9]

Here our question is: From whence came the "long forgotten specific incidents" evoked by the shouted phrase? As in the other examples, it seems highly unlikely that the brain holds permanent physicochemical capsules containing the pattern of such incidents, long buried and repressed. On the other hand, these incidents, and the visual impressions of the four-year-old Ian Hunter, and the early day-of-the-week birthday memories, and the prisoner's recollection of a childhood train conductor's call, and the childhood fairy tales of Brenman's patients—all these were retained *in some way*. We shall consider later what that way might be.

I propose now that you try a small experiment on yourself to reveal some hidden memories. Try to remember how many windows there are on the first floor of your house or in your apartment. How did you get the answer? Psychologist Ulric Neisser, who devised this experiment, suggests that if the question was new to you, you probably found the answer by counting "mental" windows.[10] If so, then here you were able to image the outer walls of various rooms in a way that you probably only rarely had occasion to do before. This suggests that far more information rests in your memory store than you ever expected to need or sought to acquire—and much of this in the "wasteful" form of imagery rather than the condensed form of an information bit (i.e., the number of windows). This "wasteful" type of image memory suggests once again that many of one's past experiences are retained, not as mere informational traces, but in the same way they were experienced. A similar view about what we are calling pure memory was advanced by the founder of psychoanalysis, Sigmund Freud.

Based on his self-analysis and his clinical experience, Freud believed that the human memory store is an influential and permanent record of our focal life events. He spelled it out as follows:

> It is highly probable that there is no question at all of there being any direct function of time in forgetting. In the case of

repressed memory-traces it can be demonstrated that they undergo no alteration even in the course of the longest period of time. The unconscious is quite timeless. The most important as well as the strangest characteristic of physical fixation is that all impressions are preserved, not only in the same form in which they were first received, but also in all the forms which they have adopted in their further developments . . . . Theoretically every earlier state of the mnemic (i.e., memory) content could thus be restored to memory again (i.e., could be recalled), even if its elements have long ago exchanged all their original connections for more recent ones.[11]

Indeed, psychoanalytic theory presupposes that early memories we have "forgotten" through repression, distortion and screening still exist, as Freud said, in our unconscious —and they can be brought to consciousness and freed of their old psychic weight (*Besetzung,* cathexis) by the right therapeutic technique. Our hidden memories, Freud also stressed, are not "objective" but represent the way things seemed to us at the time they happened.

Now Freud, in philosophy, was reductionist and materialist. However, except for one early unpublished project, he paid little attention to the specifics of brain-mind relations. Thus he offers us no real insight on *where* the pure memories dwell. Rather, he strongly asserts that they do persist, "virtually immortal," out of awareness.

If we add these findings from depth psychiatry to those from psychology, and apply also the neurological and neurophysiological findings, we have now amply confirmed the inaccuracy of the Russell-Lamont thesis that pure memories are stored in the brain. That thesis appears highly implausible. I should rank it even lower, as maximally implausible, except that the brain remains to some degree *terra incognita;* its functioning is extremely complex, and some possibility exists that a revolution may occur in our understanding of its storage capabilities. The evidence we do have, though, appears highly persuasive against the Russell-Lamont thesis that pure memories are reducible to material traces in the brain.

Correspondingly, the claim that pure memories are stored in some other way now has a high plausibility. This removes the first and heaviest empirical attack on the notion of personal survival after death. Our conclusion, however, depends on there *being* some other way to store pure memories. We shall explore that question in due course.

We now have further indications also—from the most disparate sources—to support Penfield's finding that seemingly unimportant pure memories may be stored for long periods. Moreover, these may exist quite unknown to the person's conscious mind, as it were "behind the veil." However, even if the events so retained may seem objectively unimportant, it appears likely that they were the focus of attention and interest when they occurred.

The new evidence, added to Penfield's, offers the intriguing possibility that many pure memories are stored not simply as information bits or traces but rather in something like their original perceptual form. That opens a window into the spread-out nature of personal identity, and into what personal survival might mean. A different approach to these questions, the phenomenological approach, may offer some further insights.

9

Evidence On Memory–III

Phenomenologists seek to focus on immediate, direct experience, putting aside all theories and preconceptions, and to pull from experience itself its essential structures. These investigators have devoted considerable attention to the experience of time and have inquired to a lesser degree into the recall of pure memories. The following pages will draw heavily on their memory inquiries. This review will focus on two questions important to our interest: *First, what further light does the phenomenology of memory shed on the possibility of brain storage of pure memories? Second, what light does it shed on pure memory storage requirements, however such memories are stored?*

Phenomenologists point out that in the imagery type of pure memory one is usually aware of the past as past. Remembered objects, episodes, or persons are re-presented, experienced now but as emerging from past time. This emergence becomes more full, more contextual, as we attend to the memory. And the past that emerges is not an objective physical past but is our own life history. It is personal, ours alone. It occurs, in phenomenologist Edmund Husserl's metaphor, as an "inside" track nested within the outer track of our ongoing present consciousness. We experience, less vividly, the same kind of doubling as Penfield's patients did. In Husserl's words: "I do not just exist and just live, but a second ego and a second entire life of an ego is made known, is mirrored in my life, i.e., is represented in my present remembering."[1]

This state of affairs appears to rule out the notion that imagery recall is simply a revived, less intense kind of perception. Reactivation of the brain's perceptual systems, in a way analogous to what produced the original perceptions, could not provide the experience of something emerging-from-my-own-past that we get in these recallings. We would get a new perception, not a memory, out of such a reactivation. This is an important fact. It offers a new setback to trace theories of memory storage. If pure memories are stored as traces, whether in the brain or in some other way, a simple activation of those traces could not produce the imagery we get; for a trace has attributes far different from what it signifies: the bear's footprint is his trace but it offers no picture of the bear. Thus a trace theory, to account for image memories, requires something more. That "more" would have to be reactivation of the perceptual apparatus by the stored traces, since we have no evidence of any other available image-making system. But reactivation of the perceptual apparatus does not account for the personal-pastness of much pure memory recall. The trace theory, thus, is an insufficient explanation for pure memory storage.

This leads us into asking again whether pure memories might be kept and stored *as first experienced,* without reduction to traces. An imagery recall, then, would mean that we in the present somehow pull that experience out of the past. This personal-pastward aspect of pure remembering thus diminishes further the plausibility of brain storage of such memories, in the form either of neuronal traces or of trace patterns.

Further support for the same conclusion derives from the experience of *context* in remembering. The context may involve the physical/social location of the experience one recalls (at Bethany Beach, at a brother-in-law's apartment, on one's last visit to Paris, at Gerald's cocktail party). The context may also include a sequence of events, as experienced. It may offer a conclusion based upon a certain mental arranging or weighting of the context in a remembered experience. Thus William James cites the case of our recalling that something did *not* happen, that we did not wind our watch or did not lock the door. "The image of winding the watch is just as present to my mind now when I remember that I did not wind it as if I remembered that I did," James reports. However, "when I remember that I did wind it, I feel it grown together with its associates of past date and place. When I remember that I did not, it keeps aloof; the associates fuse with each other, but not with it."[2] Thus the contents of recall (the only items that could be derived from traces) are equally present in both cases; but the cognitive feel of the image-to-context is different, completely changing the meaning.

Again, phenomenologist Robert Sokolowski cites a man who thinks back over a meeting he had with some others:

> He lets the meeting take place over and over again in his memory; suddenly he realizes, "Those two were in collusion! They were signaling to one another. Perhaps they plan to exploit the disagreements that exist among the rest of us!" He has just registered this complex fact . . . not by inference but intuitively through memory, by allowing the meaning and all the subtle parts of the events to sink in. The man actually came to see the suspects signalling to one another and making devious moves; he did not conclude inferentially that they were doing so.[3]

Here the sharp shift in meaning derives not from examining a given, limited set of traces from the past, but by vivifying, particularizing in more and more detail, an evocation of the past experience itself.

A third accompaniment to pure recalling (in addition to personal pastness and context) is often a feeling tone. If a feeling tone could be deposited as a trace, along with other aspects of a pure memory, it would have to be the feeling tone experienced at the time. In recalling, however, we often experience feelings at variance with the original. As Erwin Straus, a phenomenological psychiatrist, points out, if we suffered in the past, we may today recall those hard times with pleasure, enjoying the contrast with our present comforts.[4] We may recall the same events with varying feelings. Eugene Minkowski, another phenomenological psychiatrist, notes the sharp variations when we simply talk about what we did during the war, when we try to re-evoke our war experience or, finally, "when we feel it still present in the very fiber of our being, when we feel it thus become a part of our present even more than the actual present."[5]

The same reasoning we applied earlier to the personal pastness quality of recalling can be applied also to the varying contexts and feeling tones that go with this kind of pure memory experience. All of these aspects of remembering cast further doubt on the brain trace theory of memory storage. They cast doubt, in fact, on *any* form of trace storage for pure memories. They suggest the notion, rather, that the past as experienced may be in part preserved and drawn upon in this kind of memory—though without offering any theory as to how that might occur.

So far we have explored chiefly the imagery type of pure memory. Let us now turn briefly to the cognitive type, that is, one's remembering of insights had and facts retained. The most intriguing kinds of cognitive recall involve one's memory of concepts and propositions and their interlinkings. Philosophers differ about the status of concepts and propositions. But the term *concept* denotes, at least, the meaning (or one of the meanings) of a word. Now whether we take the meaning of a word to lie in its usage, in various experienced images, in an ideal form, or whatever, our use of this word meaningfully implies a whole set of relations remembered, out of our past experience, out of assimilated innate ideas, or possibly (if we follow Plato) out of a previous soul-life. We use a word in the present; we understand it out of the past. Likewise with propositions. They signify the meaning (or one of the meanings) of a truth-asserting sentence. People can and do express the meanings they ascribe to concepts and propositions through a wide variety of words and sentences, that is, many different sentences can signify the same proposition and many different words can define the same concept. Moreover, people interrelate words and sentences as to meanings in extremely complex patterns, and they are constantly augmenting these patterns.[6]

The point to be made here is simply that this immensely complex structure of conceptual/propositional/linguistic meanings held in our memory out of awareness, and constantly drawn on in recalling, cannot plausibly be reduced to combinations of neurons, as we have come to understand the functioning of neurons. Neuronal activations (firings) can display great complexity; but this complexity is an affair only of spatial relations in the brain-space plus temporal sequences in that same brain-space. Behind the patterns of firings lie further great complexities of electrical and biochemical nature. But none of this patterning of neurons seems comparable at all to the hypercomplex relations of *meanings* that people draw on in significant cognitive recall. Ask yourself this: Is my notion of love, which I now try to pull out of my past thoughts and experiences, reducible altogether to neuronal patterns in my brain? One set of patterns, those in the brain, carries no meaning; the other set carries meanings as its primary relations, both word meanings and life meanings. One set clearly cannot be equated with the other.

Thus we find that phenomenological analysis of pure memory, of the imagery type and of the cognitive type, yields further strong reasons for rejecting brain storage of such memories. We are confirmed even further in our conclusion that brain storage is highly implausible. We have also opened further the idea that pure memories of individual focal episodes might be held not as traces but as they were first experienced, if there is some plausible way of envisaging this. Lastly, we have touched on meanings as an aspect of experience and memory not plausibly reducible to brain action alone.

Let us now go a bit further and speculate (with many philosophers) that the past is somehow preserved and that, in recalling our pure memories, we in the present draw upon a portion of the past. Let us call the past as preserved the "real past." Now it does not seem possible that this real past should be material in nature. If it were, the physical mass/energy of the present would be constantly diminished as more and more of it became past—or, alternatively, the physical universe would have to be fed with a steadily increasing supply of mass / energy. But the principle of conservation of energy would not allow either alternative, and we have no reason to abandon that principle as applied to the closed system of the physical universe. Therefore a real past cannot be material in nature.

Is the real past objective in nature? Various idealist philosophers emphasize the objective—that is, the nonsubjective—status of the real past. With some this leads to a notion of objective immortality. But the real past, if it is the source for recall of one's pure memories, must be in relation with subjectivity; it must be reachable by one's present subjective self. But here we have made a major assumption: that each person has an active subjective self. So far, however, we have taken no serious look at the human self. The nature of the self is crucial to our inquiry into personal survival. We shall, then, postpone our ontological explorations until Part Four and turn now to examine the self. We pose two questions: *Can a plausible notion of the self be framed that will fit with what we have learned about memory? Will such a notion of the self fit plausibly also with personal survival after death?*

After developing a notion of the self in the next two chapters, we shall then examine the second great empirical objection raised by some philosophers against survival, namely, their claim of an indissoluble unity between mind and brain or between mind-brain-environment. This challenge adds intensity to our inquiry into the self. We have now found a great implausibility for the first objection, which says individual survival is impossible because each person's pure memories (and, thus, his or her identity) are imprinted in the mortal brain. But even so, if each person's self is united indissolubly to the brain or environment, then the naturalistic case for survival loses plausibility. Thus, if our inquiry is to yield a positive answer, we must develop a plausible view about the nature of the self that fits not only with our memory findings but also with the other requirements for meaningful survival.

10

Approach through the Self

From earliest times prophets and poets and philosophers have tried to analyze the nature of human be-ing.* More recently psychologists, psychiatrists, sociologists, and anthropologists have added their findings and opinions. Some have proffered a simple view. Plato compared the soul of man to "a pair of winged horses and a charioteer," one of the horses being "upright and cleanly made . . . a lover of honor and modesty and temperance," while the other is "a crooked lumbering animal" filled with lust and insolence and pride.[1] Freud, twenty-three hundred years later, favored a somewhat similar division, with a realistic ego attempting to guide a moral superego and a lustful id. Among those who prefer complex classifications, one might cite the psychologist Henry Murray. He worked up a list of twenty human needs, each one with complex definitions, which interact with sixteen kinds (and many sub-kinds) of environmental "press."[2] At the opposite extreme are radical behaviorists like B. F. Skinner who assert that, apart from the genetic code, humans have no inner nature but only a "repertoire of behavior" taught by the environment.[3]

---

*The word *being* serves as both a noun and the present participle of the verb *to be*. I shall hyphenate it, be-ing, whenever I use it as a verbal noun (gerund) to convey an activity, not a static condition.

Clearly it is no easy matter to analyze the self, which I
define as the human being viewed inwardly. We humans are
individual and changeable and immensely complex. We cannot be compressed into a single classification scheme. And yet
there are patterns and stabilities. What I propose here is a
simple diagram illustrating the self's most stable relationships. This diagram (Fig. 2) seeks to present the key structures
of the normal adult human self in the world, based on what

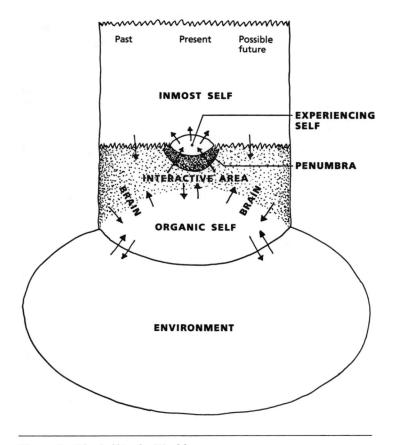

Figure 2. *The Self in the World*

we have learned so far about memory and the brain, plus other easily checkable information. The next chapter will consider the dynamic factors at work in the self. In both cases the aim is not to offer a perfect version but merely one of moderate plausibility. By this I mean that there is substantial evidence for this approach, of greater weight than any opposing evidence.

Turning now to Fig. 2, please note that, for simplicity, I have labelled as a kind of *self* what are in fact structural divisions of one self. These are not separate selves but divisions of the one whole self. Please note also that up and down, right and left, have no significance; the arrangement is wholly schematic. Taking first the diagram's lower part, the outer environment impacts on our *organic self,* which consists of the organism including the brain in its inward functioning. In the other direction, part of the organism's activity—often responding to orders from the brain—impacts on the environment. All this takes place in the physical realm, and the brain is physically in the organism which is in the environment.[4] Moreover, as shown here, the only interaction between self and environment flows through the organism. It seems plausible that this is normally true; but I do not wish to rule out all cases of extrasensory perception, which will be discussed later.

The upper part of the diagram is more unusual.[5] Our conscious *experiencing self* is the small oval set in the middle. This is drawn small for two reasons: First, our conscious experiencing, rich as it may be, does not endure long. Second, our focal experiences at any one moment, central though they are, are limited in number. Around the core of the experiencing self is a shadowy *penumbra.* This holds the background horizons currently operating behind the bright foreground of the experiencing self. This arrangement allows for the fact that we are no more than peripherally conscious or semiconscious of some of our experiencing. However, very short-term interactions of perceiving-remembering-feeling are not adequately allowed for in this simple diagram. The actual self is obviously far more complex than shown; but the diagram does present the main features of self-structure.

Our conscious experiencing self offers what Husserl called our life-world. Its contents come and go so quickly that they rarely ʒet described. How extraordinary this flow of experience is—the sudden surprising shifts, the logical jumps, the sights, the scents and sounds, the worries, the hop into memory and out again, the skip into imagined adventures and back again, the interpretations, illusions, checked-up-on impressions, the feelings, startlements, longings and lustings. Above all else, here everything revolves around *meaning.* If meaning fails immediately to clothe a percept, then the mind tries on one possible meaning or another until one fits or until (so quickly!) life thrusts this mystery aside.

What we are dealing with here is a world none of us could grasp at all if we did not ourselves experience it. It is the direct immediate world known to each of us. This is the world of the experiencing self.

Many focal events of the experiencing self feed into the *inmost self.* The inmost self thus holds our long-term pure memories. Indeed, since we concluded that these memories are not stored in the brain, I have simply labeled "inmost self" the part of the self that holds them. Three temporal words are used to suggest that the inmost self has a temporal spread of some kind. This seems implied by the fact that pure memories are, in many cases, arranged sequentially; but I also have other reasons for the suggestion, as will appear. Notable activity occurs in the inmost self, including creative thinking and willing, as we shall also see. While the experiencing self alone is conscious, let us call the inmost self superconscious, the penumbra foreconscious, and the interactive area subconscious.[6]

The *interactive area,* where brain and mind interact, occupies a key position. Note that activity can flow from the interactive area through the penumbra to the experiencing self, then to the inmost self, but not in the reverse direction. Thus all normal information reaches the inmost self only through the conscious experiencing self, including some information that passes through the experiencing self without being overtly attended to there. Also, willed decisions from the inmost self in some cases proceed directly through the interactive area to the organic self. We then find ourselves starting to act before we are aware that we had decided to do so.

Equally important, information from the inmost self can reach our conscious awareness only after passing through the interactive area. This area fulfills an important guardian function. It blocks off many brain stimuli from consciousness. As neurophysiologist Sir John Eccles reports, "by far the greater part of the activity of the brain, and even in the cerebral cortex, does not reach consciousness at all."[7] The interactive area also blocks out of consciousness many memories and thoughts from the inmost self that might confuse us. However, this area may also repress, screen, or distort—because of past emotions or present ambivalences— some things that we truly need to bring into awareness. Here we find the repressor systems stressed by Freud. This explains the many blockages and distortions we encounter when we try to bring our pure memories or our inner goals fully into consciousness.

One can view the interactive area as embracing the higher electrochemical systems of the brain, with added "staff work" by a complex variety of mental systems. These brain-mind systems, or schemata, in a rising hierarchy, include the apparatus for converting neuronal sense data (or their average patterns) into conscious percepts, and organic tensions into conscious feelings. They include the apparatus for "reading" stimuli and generating organic responses, and also for conveying orders from the inmost self to the brain. Interactive area schemata include our habit memories. They include skill programs such as speech,[8] tool using, writing, driving, playing instruments and sports. They include affect programs that stimulate or repress our feelings based on learned patterns.

And the *inmost self?* What else can we say about it, apart from its function as holder of pure memories? First this: The inmost self also holds one of the great omissions from the diagram, the self as subject. We have considered events, experiencings, schemata, activities of the self, but where is the

"I" who is the subject for all this? Oneself as subject is the I meant when one says "I decided not to take the job" or "I hate spiders" or "I know I'm stubborn" or "I loved her for three years but I couldn't care less about her now." This subjective I isn't one's organism, nor one's conscious experiences, nor one's subconscious mental operations. Those are all objects or activities, whereas this I is always a subject. A fleeting, even vanishing, subject. Whenever one tries to bring this I into awareness, it turns into an "I felt this" or an "I did that," thus into a subject-object combination, and thereby in one's awareness it always becomes a past event or intentional object, a subject no longer.

We thus return to Hume's dilemma, discussed in Chapter Four. But now, with the self-structure proposed here, we do (unlike Hume) have a home for the subjective I. This I spreads itself through the inmost self, always aware of the conscious experiencing self but never in it. The only alternative location—in the interactive area—is not plausible. If the subjective I were in the interactive area, along with all the sense data and schemata, it would have to be either (1) available for grasping by the experiencing self, like the other objects of awareness, or (2) if not so available, then impacting on experience only as a subject-object combination. Actually, however, the subjective I is neither graspable in experience nor merely one part of a combination. As we noted, the I is beyond the experiencing self. It is the most extensive yet the most intimate reality of selfhood. It is the subject of personal identity, whose contents, as we saw, comprise largely one's pure memories, held in the inmost self. For these reasons it seems highly plausible that the subjective I operates from the inmost self. How it functions there will be explored later. For the present we turn to the dynamics of self.

11

Dynamics of the Self

We can best understand what moves the self, as it deals with the world outside and within, if we group its motive forces in three ascending and interacting levels. Each level has its own characteristic thirst.* We shall call these levels the somatic, the hedonic, and the noetic.

The somatic level moves by thirst for life. Here is the basic dimension found in all living creatures, plant and animal alike. By life, as Aristotle says, "we mean self-nutrition and growth (with its correlative decay)."[1] These two, with reproduction, are the somatic tasks. Such tasks you and I share with a rosebush, an ant, a bacterium, a salmon. The thrust behind them was named by Bergson *elan vital* and placed at

---

*Both *force* and *thirst* are used metaphorically in denoting the dynamics of human motives. They, and especially *thirst,* seem more useful than other possible terms, all of which suffer from serious drawbacks. Thus *interaction* is too broad and loses the essence of what-moves-us. *Motive* suggests what already knows its object; whereas what-moves-us may not yet have found an object. Other metaphorical terms, such as *tension, valence, need,* or the Greek *love* and *hate,* are also very broad and have other conflicting uses. *Thirst,* by contrast, has a strong clear meaning in ordinary usage, and this meaning carries over well into the powerful but not-always-directed essence of what-moves-us. Each thirst, in expression, becomes a force.

the core of his philosophy. Sir Charles Sherrington, an English physiologist, called it a zest to live:

> At once an urge and a motive. No species of life without it. Innate, inalienable, impelling alike man and animalcule . . . . It was panegyrized years ago as will-to-live. But that was a misconception . . . As well call an ocean-tide which sweeps the mariner onward his "will." As well suppose we summon the Spring's growth by asking for it. To think of the vast nether flood of urge-to-live as mere will-to-live is to miss the meaning of the whole subconscious world whence man has come, and in part still belongs . . . . I remember sowing into two litres of distilled water—contained in one of a pair of similarly filled tall glass jars—a minute speck of a culture of cholera germ. I added this speck to the clear water just before leaving the laboratory late on the summer afternoon. Next forenoon, to my extreme astonishment, the whole tall column of water in the one jar was faintly opalescent. I microscoped a drop. It teemed with myriads of cholera germs, the progeny of my speck of the day before. An almost incredible multiplication.[2]

This life-thirst, by the time it reaches man, has spawned a complex web of needs. These are handled in part by the organism's basic action and regulatory systems—homeostatic, reflexive, and instinctive. The somatic force thrusts also into the subconscious interactive area. In the brain one might speculate, with the neurologist Paul MacLean, that the primal life-thirst operates from the "reptilian" level, the genetically oldest part of the brain.[3]

In the evolutionary scale this protoplasmic thirst precedes not only conscious awareness but also pleasure-pain. It underlies all that we do and much that we feel. Usually we are not aware of the primal life-force at all. It is our silent servant. It makes itself known to consciousness—when frustrated—through mediation of the next higher level, the hedonic. Thus when our organic self needs food, this fact reaches our conscious experiencing self as a feeling of distress that we label hunger (unless the message has been garbled or diverted). But eventually, in all sexually reproducing species, the life force dwindles and the organism dies. This thirst for life, therefore, cannot accompany us beyond the grave.

The self's second dynamic level we shall call hedonic. It moves by thirst for pleasure. More exactly it seeks pleasure and flees distress. This is close to Freud's pleasure principle. Pleasure can be defined ostensively as agreeable affect: experiencing the enjoyable emotions and feelings. No doubt this is often associated with a well-paced reduction of organic tensions. MacLean proposes, based on substantial evidence, that the brain's limbic system plays a major transmissive role in this.[4] Psychologists Henry Murray and Clyde Kluckhohn make a further important point: "It is not a tensionless state, as Freud supposed, which is generally most satisfying to a healthy organism, but the *process* of reducing tension." A tensionless state, they argue, is sometimes the ideal of "those who suffer from chronic anxiety or resentment or a frustrated sex drive; but, as a rule, the absence of positive need-tensions —no appetite, no curiosity, no desire for fellowship, no zest —is very distressing."[5]

The opposite of pleasure on the hedonic scale is best called distress, not pain. That is because it may reach us not only as pain but as fear, dread, anxiety, anguish, strain, suppressed emotion, and even boredom. Feelings of pleasure or distress, mild or intense, attach themselves to our perceptions, our imaginings, our rememberings, our resolves. In this way, as Freud pointed out, the hedonic force greatly influences the motions and shaping of the self. At its harshest, the thirst for pleasure (and against distress) acts as a repressive censor and punisher. At its best it lifts us into hope, courage, and delight. It may also permeate the whole penumbra of our awareness, setting our mood.

In MacLean's words, the "raw stuff of the affects" (that is, our pleasure thirst) is probably built into the limbic system of the brain. Dynamically, the force of the pleasure thirst operates most sweepingly in the interactive area, fixating many of our subconscious schemata with its own positive or negative charge. This charge is not in itself a feeling or emotion. Feelings and emotions must normally be conscious, as noted by Freud.[6] They come only through the experiencing self. But the hedonic charge, positive or negative, underlies them. As for the situation beyond death, if the hedonic charge is tied to the brain, it could not survive the brain's destruction. We shall consider in Part Four what this may imply for any postmortem feelings.

At the noetic level—in our experiencing and our inmost self—we come upon a third dynamic factor. This is the thirst for meaning. Here we operate with new contents, including pure memories, and use the broad new field of conscious and superconscious awareness. What is meaning? It is a completion. It is grasping something as a whole, knowing its inward relations and qualities. Equally, meaning is grasping something as a part, knowing it as participating in larger and ever larger wholes. Meaning also involves acceptance or rejection, and thus reflection: an I-object awareness or an I-thou awareness. When the acceptance of meaning is conscious, it often comes as a flash of insight, an illumination, an intuition. The whole set of such meanings composes our personal identity in its inwardness.* Seeking for meaning, the subjective I in the inmost self uses thought, imagination, will, and judgment. But we shall postpone examining these noetic powers and turn once again to consider the critics of survival. The reason for doing so now is this:

We have found strong evidence that many pure memories are preserved, and great implausibility for the view that they are stored in the brain. Thus we conclude that pure memories are held in some other mode. Building on this memory in-

---

*The person-that-I-am inwardly is, of course, different from the person-that-I-am to others, e.g., to my wife, my employer, my church, the state. I have used *meaning* in this discussion much more broadly than linguistic philosophers do. *Meaning* here includes not only the sense and reference of words and concepts, but also the valuation of experiences, goals, and ideas. This builds upon our pure memories.

Also, the dynamics of the self produce conflicts as well as harmonies. Indeed, the balance may be so shifted at times that one of the great thirsts is negated. The individual desires or acts for death, not life; for distress, not pleasure; for *anomie,* not meaning. In such cases the two non-negated thirsts may have combined in a pattern that overcomes and negates the third one. Thus heavy blows to the meaning structure of one's life may make one imagine suicide with pleasure, and perhaps even do the act.

quiry and on other evidence, we developed a proposal for the structure and dynamics of the self. With this proposal an obvious possibility opens up. *At death, when the organic self and its life-thirst perish, the whole self might split apart at the interactive level.* Given that the inmost self with its pure memories exists in a different mode from the brain, no logic requires that it dissolve with the brain. Indeed, at death the experiencing self might pull back into the inmost self, and thereafter the noetic inmost-experiencing self, with its memories, knowledge, feelings, and meanings, its spreading subjective I, might persist indefinitely. Of course we do not yet see clearly how this could occur, nor what really goes on in the inmost self, nor what mode of being it has. Yet this scenario does seem newly *possible.* This is not so, however, in the view of some thinkers. These thinkers hold that our line of reasoning mistakes the whole nature of what it is to be human. We have already met with this argument in Chapter Four, where I suggested that the argument needed to be considered empirically. We now have enough background to do that, and so we shall.

12

Survival and the Social Web

We now consider the claim, aired briefly in Chapter Four, that the idea of individual survival mistakes what it is to be human. First we shall examine the view that being human is founded in the social environment and therefore humans cannot survive death. Later we shall review the assertion that one's mind is either identical with or depends upon the brain and therefore it cannot survive death.

On the first issue let us turn anew to Phillips, who writes: ". . . unless there were a common life which people share, which they were taught and came to learn, there could be no notion of a person." This being so, he argues, what it means to be a person "cannot be divorced or abstracted from these common features of human life." A similar argument is advanced by Lamont, who stresses the "indissoluble connection between each individual and "the sustaining and conditioning environment, both human and physical."[1]

Now there is considerable truth in what Phillips and Lamont are saying. Each of us since arriving in the world has had to learn an extraordinary number of socially taught and socially formed ways of behaving. We learn how to speak, control our functions, use a cup, use a spoon, then knife and fork, carry things, kiss and hug, get dressed, climb stairs, tie shoelaces, read, write, "behave," prevaricate, play games,

65

make friends, fight, figure numbers . . . and so on and on, even unto now. All these skills help to shape what we are.

Moreover, society has for us the look of objective reality. The child comes into an everyday world where many rules are fixed. He or she must learn and use them. One learns one's parents' language, number system, ways of dress, manners and customs. One enters into a name and family, present and past. As one grows one learns behavior rules of school, peer groups, courting, work, money, church, citizenship, ownership, marriage, and parenthood. Society appears as a great web of manners, rules, institutions, and activities—all objectively there, offering shelters, opportunities, threats, but always *there*. These, too, shape each of us as we develop. And so with the physical environment and with the other persons to whom we relate.

Does this social web determine all that we are as humans? That seems to be a tempting view among some recent philosophers. In this view the social web, expressed largely through language games, makes up the human form of life: for us humans, all meaning filters through the web, and what does not filter through is forever unknowable. A Hegelian might say that we elevate a few aspects of Spirit to the fullness of the Absolute. Today, though, one absorbs this notion not via Hegel but from Wittgenstein and his followers, or perhaps from various psychologists, all of whom examine activity in the social web and find only *behavior*.

Despite its wide appeal, the social web argument against survival has serious weaknesses. One of these is logical. Lamont and Phillips speak of an "indissoluble" or "inextricable" linking of person and environment. Wittgenstein and others of the social web school seem to hold similar views.[2] One might frame their major premise as follows: Wherever humans develop, they do so in a social-institutional-physical environment. Minor premise: There is no such environment after death. Conclusion: Therefore, humans cannot exist after death. This is a syllogism of the form: If A, then B; not B; therefore not A. That is a valid form, but in this case the A of the major premise (human development in the ordinary mode) differs from the A of the conclusion (human existence in any mode). Therefore the syllogism is faultily constructed. This fault becomes grave when we note that we are dealing here, not with the timeless world of classical logic, but with the mode of existence of living creatures.

In the temporal world of living creatures, environment E may be necessary to the development of A at time T_1. But at a later time, T_2, the same creature A may continue to develop outside of environment E. Consider the tadpole who must grow in water; when he changes into a frog he can live also on land. Or consider the caterpillar who moults, becoming a butterfly and then takes wing. The most obvious and relevant case, however, involves the human embryo. Each of us needed our mother's womb for about nine months. Then we entered a wholly different environment. Womb life, so warm and snug, had to be abandoned. This new environment, this being-in-the-world, nourished our organic, experiencing, and inmost selves. Without it, we could not have survived and become as we are. But now a third environment may lie ahead: *survival of the inmost self in its own mode or realm*. No logic offered by the social web school has exploded that claim. Nothing in reason or experience refutes it.

Nothing in *experience* . . . But psychologists have placed people in low-stimulus environments and evoked confusion, hallucinations, and regression. Secret police agents have used a similar technique on prisoners. Doesn't this suggest that removal of the usual social-natural stimuli at death will lead to mental disintegration rather than coherent survival? Not necessarily. The low-stimulus or sensory-deprivation environments, here and now, disturb the organism's rhythms and the interactive area's habitual functioning. After death, with no organism and no interactive area, such disturbances can scarcely occur.

Along this line, a striking view on the stages of being-human has been offered by Gustav Fechner, a nineteenth century physiologist who was one of the founders of experimental psychology. As Fechner saw it:

> Man lives on earth not once but three times: the first stage of his life is continual sleep; the second, sleeping and waking by

turns; the third, waking forever . . . . In the first stage his
body develops itself from its germ, working out organs for the
second; in the second stage his mind develops itself from its
germ, working out organs for the third; in the third the divine
germ develops itself, which lies hidden in every human mind,
to direct him . . . to the world beyond . . . . The act of leaving
the first stage for the second we call birth; that of leaving the
second for the third, death.[3]

Thus, despite the arguments of the social web theorists,
survival remains logically *possible*. But their case against survival becomes *implausible* when we consider the empirical evidence about the self.

After weighing the facts about memory, we concluded
earlier that each individual retains many long-term pure
memories, out of conscious awareness, and that brain storage
of these memories is highly implausible. They are evidently
stored in another way, not in the brain. Now it seems equally
implausible that my pure memories are stored in the social
web, for they would then be regularly available to others as
well as to me; but they are not normally so available. We have
therefore posited an inmost self in each individual, which
holds his or her pure memories (and which, as later chapters
will show, is also active in mental operations). Now, since the
memory-holding inmost self is distinct from the brain and distinct also from the social web—to a high degree of plausibility—it becomes implausible that all of what I am is inextricably bound to the social web. Most of what I am has been
shaped by my lifelong interchanges with other people and
with social realities, in and through the social web. But *the
self that I am, the identity that I hold to (largely founded in
memories), is not empirically reducible to an item in the
social, or natural, environment.* My pure memories are not
held in the social web, nor in my brain; and they, along with
their interrelations, form the chief contents of my inmost self.
Thus the social web argument against survival fails on both
logical and empirical grounds.

Two further points should be noted, however. First, what
we can learn directly about other people normally comes
to us through the social web, by way of their behavior. But

this does not mean, as claimed by some philosophers and psychologists, that what we can learn directly about other people is all that they significantly amount to. People have a meaningful inward life as well as expressive outward behavior. One can argue this by analogy from oneself; like all contingent statements it is not certainly true, but one's experience with other people over many years makes it a highly plausible belief. Nor can we plausibly conclude, as suggested by some social web philosophers, that introspection disproves any serious inward activity of mind. This introspective critique runs about as follows: When I decided to lift my finger just now, I observed what went on inside and found nothing, I simply lifted my finger; therefore, deciding is not a separate mental act. So, too, with understanding, intending, and so on. This approach has a threefold weakness. (1) Trivial motions like lifting a finger offer a poor test of the mind's activity. Such notions normally form a small part of larger schemata; the mind normally becomes active as agent only in initiating and regulating those larger schemata. (2) Different people vary greatly in their ability to introspect and in the vividness of their conscious life. Therefore, one philosopher's meager introspective results may apply for him alone or for a small minority. (3) Most of the contents and activity of the mind remain out of consciousness; to get at them we must use not only inner observation but also hypothetico-deductive and experimental procedures. Thus even the best introspection cannot justify negative general assertions about the mind. One can reasonably conclude from all this that behaviorism offers no plausible challenge to survival.

Second, any argument for survival faces the old warning, "You can't take it with you." The social web is more for us than simply a world-out-there. So, too, with some parts of the world of things, especially our belongings. Our body, first of all, is our own property. Our other properties, too, are not only our own but they seem to extend our self. Thus our clothes, our room, furniture, car, tools, pets, our creations and productions, our business—in short, whatever tangible things, down to a toothbrush, that we feel as belonging intimately to ourself do broaden and strengthen our sense of solid existence. Socially, we are extended by ties to parents, spouse, children, other close relatives. Each of these persons becomes part of our life, a cause of joy or suffering, an object of love, sympathy, pride, and sometimes scalding hate. So, too, with friends, lovers, and with any we may see as enemies. Indeed our existence broadens out to relations with all other people, groups, and institutions whose attitudes and actions make a difference to us. We hold, too, as part of our life, both rights and obligations. Perhaps a separate term is needed to include what we are as a participant in the social web, as a publicly observable behavioral agent, as a human-in-relation to all these other entities, as the locus of rights and duties. The word *person* can be used to embrace both this public aspect of being human and also the inward aspect. The word *self,* then, will refer only to what one is inwardly. And for personal identity as experienceable by oneself, we shall use the term *selfhood.*

So how much *can* we carry beyond the grave? In the public aspect of "person," what one is as a person evidently dies with one's organism, except referentially. Does this mean that what one *has been* as a participating person will perish as well? We shall examine that in Part Four. We might also ask how much of a person's inward self could survive. Isn't the whole of the self identical with or dependent upon the brain, and therefore doomed to die with the brain? We turn now to that question.

13

Survival and the Brain

Based on experience and research, nothing could appear more obvious than the interaction of mind and organism. From stimuli in our sense organs and our brains, perceptions emerge in our minds. So, too, with feelings. If the temperature of our organism drops, we feel cold; if it rises, we feel hot. If we ingest a mood drug affecting the brain, we feel high or low or relaxed or alert. Some drugs promote hallucinations; others may curb them. Organic tensions may pull our thoughts toward sex or food or drink. Physical illness may drive our mind nearly to distraction—or put us to sleep.

In the other direction, if we decide to switch on the electric light, our limbs obey. If we decide to whistle a tune, the sounds emerge from our mouth. If we desire to hug our spouse, we can usually achieve it. Our willing can even influence our heartbeat or brainwaves, through biofeedback. Anxiety of mind can open the way to physical ailments. On the other hand, one's inner self may struggle unavailingly with the organism's addictions. Indeed the struggle against bad habits displays the mind-body interaction with pathetic starkness. When we fail, how weak we feel, and then how the excuses come! Sometimes the long resolve does win through, but only after many alarms and mental barricades against the sly, swift motions of the organism in its addictive thrust.

So we experience both cooperation and struggle between the mental and organic parts of our self. There seem to be strong interactions between mind and brain (as the organism's control center), judging by human experience. But the truth about this relationship has been a perennial puzzle. The philosopher C. D. Broad, in his classic work on the subject, distinguished no less than seventeen different types of theory about the relation of mind and matter. These fall into four classes: all is basically reducible to mind, or to matter, or to some neutral stuff, or a basic dualism obtains between mind and matter.[1] Here we shall not discuss pure mentalism (panpsychism) or the "neutral stuff" theory. These two seem to me somewhat implausible as ontologies but compatible with survival; thus if either turned out to be correct, the case for survival would carry its full weight. The two more interesting approaches, from our standpoint, are reductive materialism and interactionist dualism. In the brain/mind perspective, reductive materialism holds that all mental events are either identical with brain events or dependent on them. Interactionist dualism holds that brain and mind are fundamentally different but they interact during our lives. The materialist view would rule out survival, except by miracle. *Interactionist dualism, if true, makes survival naturalistically possible, though it is not in itself evidence for survival.*

Before discussing the rivalry between these two views, let us consider briefly another form of dualism, known as epiphenomenalism. This theory holds that the brain creates the mind's conscious experiences, but those experiences play no role in nature. Our actions in the world, in this view, are functions wholly of brain and organism; consciousness is a flower with no practical use. Epiphenomenalism faces many of the same factual difficulties we shall find in reductive materialism. In addition, anyone who thinks of humans as having developed through neo-Darwinian evolution will find it hard to believe that the rich and extraordinary capacities of our conscious minds evolved with no natural function. As the philosopher of science Karl Popper puts it: "The mental system has, clearly, its evolutionary and functional history, and its functions have increased with the evolution from lower to higher organisms. It thus has to be linked with the Darwinian point of view. But epiphenomenalism cannot do this."[2]

By contrast, as noted above, interactionist dualism seems to fit with human experience. However, major arguments have been raised against it and in favor of materialism. In order to assess its plausibility, we shall now consider four of these, which seem the most widespread and interesting. This discussion is based on the views of various philosophers and, while not technical, requires rather close attention to the arguments.

1. *Energy Argument.* It is said that the causation of one event by another implies a transfer of energy. But no energy can be transferred from the physical realm to a purely mental realm. Moreover, such a leaking out of physical energy would violate the principle of conservation of energy.

However, the principle of conservation of energy applies only to closed physical systems. The question we are considering is whether human existence is an open system, with physical-mental interactions. One cannot deduce the right answer by asserting a principle that already assumes the answer (namely, that we are dealing with a closed physical system). This is simply begging the question.

Nor is it true that the cause relation necessarily involves a transfer of energy. The whole question of causality is clouded, to say the least. However, philosopher Curt Ducasse's view seems as plausible as any when he suggests that "causation of a physical by a psychical event, or of a psychical event by stimulation of a physical sense organ, is not in the least paradoxical." The causality relation, he argues, "does not presuppose at all that its cause-term and its effect-term both belong to the same ontological category, but only that both of them be events."[3]

Finally, some thinkers have suggested that mental activity may in fact use a fifth basic force, capable of interacting with the four basic forces now identified by physicists (electromagnetic, gravitational, strong nuclear, weak nuclear). No such basic mental force has been established, but neither had the two nuclear forces until a few decades ago. Any contrary assertion—namely, that the whole of reality is a closed physical system or that the whole of reality contains only four basic forces—seems a matter of faith, not of science. We can reasonably conclude that the transfer-of-energy argument to refute mind/brain interaction has little force.

2. *Incoherence Argument.* It is said that the dualist thesis traces back to Descartes and that Cartesian ideas about mind and body are clearly erroneous. Thus Descartes identified the mind as an unextended substance that thinks and the body as a machine extended in space. Descartes and his followers, the objectors say, thereby foisted on us the useless and incoherent notion of the person as a "ghost in the machine."[4]

However, whether or not the objectors are right about Descartes, in our inquiry we have found no need to speak of the mind as unextended—indeed, one's perceptions and mental images are very often extended, as Hume pointed out. Whether this extension is in physical space is another question but we have found no need for the term *substance*. Thus the anti-Cartesian argument, so far as our interest here is concerned, goes wide of the mark.

3. *Identity Argument.* It is said that mental states and mental activity are by no means irreducibly different from brain states. Rather, according to philosopher David Armstrong, a leading advocate of the brain/mind identity theory of "central state" materialism, "on this theory the mind is simply the central nervous system, or, less accurately but more epigrammatically, the mind is simply the brain."[5]

Armstrong argues that dualism is highly implausible since (1) "it seems increasingly likely that biology is completely reducible to physics," and (2) the dualist must therefore claim that the whole natural world contains nothing but "physical things operating according to the laws of physics *with the exception of mind.*"

On the empirical side, Armstrong affirms the existence of mental states but argues at length that a mental state is simply "a state of the person apt for bringing about certain sorts of (physical) behaviour." Moreover, he says, "the identification of these states with physicochemical states of the brain is, in the present state of knowledge, nearly as good a bet as the identification of the gene with the DNA molecule.'"[6]

However, Armstrong's argument to the implausibility of dualism appears much overstated. To suggest that the whole world of nature is reducible to the laws of physics implies that if we know the laws of physics we could predict the whole course of organic evolution. There is no evidence whatever to support this claim. However, hidden within this excessive claim lie the two most telling arguments against dualism, which we shall mention below.

Armstrong's empirical arguments also appear weak. On mental states, we have already reviewed much evidence on pure memories. Consider all that we have discovered about the long retention of some past experiences: how they were revived with Penfield's patients, with some people under hypnosis, with psychoanalysis, by psychologist Ian Hunter on returning to a school he last saw at the age of four. Consider that the neurophysiologists have been unable to find any brain location for such memories, nor have brain injuries destroyed them. Consider, too, the phenomenology of pure memories—their personal pastness, shifting contexts, and variable attached feeling tones—none of which fits with the brain trace theory of memory. These facts alone refute reductive materialism as to our pure memories and, thus, as to our selfhood. Moreover, these long-term memories clearly cannot be reduced to varieties of dispositional aptness for evoking physical behavior. They may be less than that, for they are often relevant to past behavior only, and also more than that, for they may carry important life meanings. So, too, with many other mental events, from simple day-dreaming to the noblest creative insights. Some of these will be described in Part Three.

Furthermore, Armstrong's aptness-to-evoke-behavior description of mental states becomes quite incredible as soon as we try to fit it to cases. Armstrong himself seems chary of offering examples, but he does mention one case of belief, while discussing behaviorism, as follows: "To believe that the earth is flat is to be disposed to carry out certain bodily actions: uttering, and speaking in defense of, the statement 'the earth is flat,' and many similar things.'''[7] Now the key point here is that the aptness for behavior involved in this belief—and in any other general belief—is not an aptness to utter one particular sentence or do one particular thing but to do any of hundreds or thousands of such acts, depending on the circumstances. Thus if the mental state of believe-the-earth-is-flat consists in being apt to behave in certain ways, and if all of this exists in the brain, then this one belief consists of many hundreds or thousands of separate action programs stored in the person's neurons.[8]

Now let us recall that the brain is constantly active; that it seems impossible to evoke any single response regularly from any small group of neurons; that much of the cerebral cortex is committed to processing sense data and motoric innervations and to other habitual activities; that aptness-to-behave involves not only habitual actions but countless new modes of expression (in expounding or defending "the earth is flat," for example); that this applies to most of our myriad different beliefs, and to our perceivings and rememberings and decidings and other mental states. For Armstrong, each of these must carry with it, in the brain, what it really *is,* namely, a whole array of "aptivated" neuronal action programs. This picture seems highly implausible, but it is implied by Armstrong's version of the identity theory: for any other view of what he says would separate our mental states from the brain neurons and thus abandon identity.[9]

But no matter how implausible, we should look at Armstrong's empirical evidence for his reductionist view. Unfortunately he has not offered any. Despite his comparing the likelihood of his view with the identification of the genome and DNA (for which we do have ample evidence), Armstrong presents not a shred of empirical data identifying any mental state with any brain state. Of course, we do have substantial evidence showing a close relation between certain mental states and brain activity, but this relation can easily be interpreted causally rather than as identity.

All these reasons suffice to refute the effort by Armstrong and others to replace dualistic interactionism with a brain/ mind identity theory. Upon examination, their approach is highly implausible.[10]

4. *Emergence Argument.* Inadequacies in the traditional reductivist view have led Roger W. Sperry, a Nobel Prize-winning psychobiologist, to offer a theory he calls emergent interactionism. This has gained widespread support among neuroscientists.[11]

Sperry claims to avoid both reductionism and dualism. "The reductionist approach that would always explain the whole in terms of the parts," he warns, "leads to an infinite nihilistic regress in which eventually everything is held to be explainable in terms of essentially nothing." Sperry proposes that mental phenomena consist of "dynamic holistic properties" that emerge in the higher levels of brain activity. Conscious experiences—and therefore human values—play a causal role in the world, he affirms. He finds "a mutual interdependence" between the neural events and the emergent mental phenomena. Thus, he writes, "the brain physiology determines the mental effects, and the mental phenomena in turn have causal influence on the neurophysiology." This means, among other things, that "values of all kinds, even aesthetic, spiritual, and irrational, must now be recognized as positive causal factors per se in human decision-making."[12]

So far this suggests a causal interactionism, as follows: A certain neural state, NS_1, causes an emergent conscious state, CS_1. Previously developed values (which are now remembered? Sperry says nothing about memory) are applied to CS_1, leading to CS_2, a decision. CS_2 then causes NS_2, activation of the decision. Here an identity theorist would posit that CS_1, CS_2 and the remembered values are all simply other sets of neural states. Sperry claims to reject this sort of reductionism. He also rejects "various sophistries and epistemological gymnastics that would make it [the brain/mind issue] just a pseudo-problem." Thus one would expect him to hold that CS_1, CS_2, the remembered values—and, in fact, consciousness as a whole—have an existence distinct from brain activity. Instead, however, Sperry affirms that "the subjective conscious experience on these terms becomes an integral part of the brain process."[13]

If we take this last expression literally, Sperry seems to plunge us back into the reductionist pit. But Sperry's view needs to be understood in the light of how parts and wholes operate in living systems. As the biologist Paul A. Weiss puts it: "Living nature . . . reveals itself to be ordered hierarchically in descending steps from supersystems through systems to subsystems, and so on down through different orders of magnitude and levels of system stability, with jumps through unstable conditions between levels."[14] Sperry finds a similar hierarchy in the brain, with each lower system being superseded or encompassed by the holistic properties of the next higher system. At the apex, he writes, "are the large cerebral processes that mediate mental activity."[15] Here Sperry seems to propose that mental activity depends on the cerebral processes in the way a whole depends on its parts. But this is just what we have found reason to doubt. At the top level of the human self the brain does not plausibly hold, as parts or otherwise, the mind's pure memories, its values (as concepts), or various other mental powers that will be explored in succeeding chapters. Thus Sperry's view does not account well for key persistent aspects of mind.

Nonetheless Sperry's emergent interactionism seems the most plausible alternative to dualistic interactionism. It builds on a telling criticism of the dualist approach to mind, namely, that we find in all living creatures a hierarchy of systems with holistic properties, but all of these depend for their existence on their subordinate parts: so why should the human mind be different and separable from its brain? Yet if our mind, or most of it, is not so separable, then any hope of a naturalistic survival after death will vanish.

The dualist can respond that man is not the only creature with a mind of sorts, and that some animal minds might also be distinct and separable from their brains. Instead of pressing this point, however, we here shall explore various capacities of the inmost self to find how plausible it is that these capacities depend wholly on the brain. This will be the chief inquiry in Part Three.

A second telling criticism of interactionist dualism is a deep skepticism, even bewilderment, about the notion that the world could contain human selves as immaterial entities. This challenge will be examined in Part Four.

III

Mind in Action

14

What We Seek Here

We now must ask ourselves: What does survival after death really amount to? So far, we have found it highly plausible that pure memories are stored otherwise than in the brain. We have labeled the part of the self holding pure memories as the superconscious inmost self and speculated that this may split off from the brain at death. But what goes on in the inmost self? Is it active or passive? Up to now we have seen the inmost self only as a passive storehouse for memories. Evidence exists that it is also highly active and productive. The following chapters will seek to weigh some of this evidence.

If this claim of an active, creative inmost self *cannot* be supported, then the survival hypothesis loses most of its value. For consider the alternatives: One cannot plausibly assert that all mental activity takes place in the conscious experiencing self. On the contrary, as many psychologists and philosophers and poets have pointed out, much of our mental life unrolls unconsciously. In Goethe's words, "Man cannot persist long in a conscious state, he must throw himself into the unconscious, for his root lives there."[1]

If this unconscious mental activity depends on neuronal patterns in the brain, even holistic patterns, then what becomes of the survival hypothesis? In that case, all that remains of us in the realm beyond the grave is the vast store of our pure memories, inactive, archival, dead leaves of vanished years. If memories alone survive in this realm—without activity—then we might as well perish fully, after our organism goes. What value of selfhood would remain with only the pressed leaves of memory and no recalling or comparing or judging or understanding or enjoying? An after-life of that slim kind would amount to very little, for the individual as a self and for those who have gone before.

Moreover, this reduction of all unconscious mental activity to brain-tied systems pulls the whole of our present existence down to a flat-life reality, a here-and-now kind of living, squeezing us into a this-moment-only flatness between an archival past and an unattained future. Indeed this is the kind of be-ing that much of the intellectual-scientific establishment would impose on humankind. They have built a reductionist trap with the best will in the world but with too narrow a view of reality. Their view shrinks each individual person into a momentary basic reality (physical organism) and a host of shadows (all the rest of life). In fact, not one of us does act or exist merely as an organism plus shadows. But to justify a full-life belief, we must explore what happens in the inmost self. We must ask whether all unconscious operations can plausibly be tied to brain functioning—or whether there is not, in fact, a fully active mind at work superconsciously. How can we find out?

We shall have to deduce an answer, based on what is the most plausible nonconscious source for some of our conscious experiences. Our method will be as follows: We start with the conscious experiencings. We assume that every experience has an explanation, that is, some reason or reasons for its occurring as it did. This postulate of sufficient reason is fundamental for any scientific or philosophical investigation. At times we are unable to deduce a coherent explanation for a particular event. Then we are forced to ascribe the event to "chance" or, as we say, to an accident. When we seek to explain an experience, the source of its primary explanation, whether coherent or accidental, may lie in the brain or in the interactive area (that is, in brain-tied subconscious systems) or in the inmost self (that is, in the nonconscious area where our pure memories are lodged, apart from the brain, as we concluded earlier).

In our present inquiry, if we are to explain certain conscious experiences by prior activity in the inmost self, then we shall need criteria which plausibly rule out both the brain and the interactive area as the explanatory source. As for explanation through chance or accident, such occurrences may well happen in the brain or the interactive area, for example, accidental neuronal firings or chance triggering of a subconscious schema. So our criteria must also rule out chance or accident as the plausible explanation for those experiences whose source we ascribe to activity in the inmost self.

We shall use three criteria, taken together, as indicators that inmost self activity is the plausible explanation for a particular experience. First, *when pure memories come into play in generation of an experience, the inmost self is presumably involved,* for "inmost self" is the name we have given to that portion of the self that holds our pure memories, distinct from the brain.

Second, as we noted at the end of Chapter Ten, the inmost self seems the only plausible home for the subjective I, the I that is always a subject and never an object, the I that holds my identity, shaped and formed in major part out of the long sequence of my pure memories. As indicated briefly in Chapter Eleven, and as shown by phenomenological reflection, the subjective I is also the part of the self that seeks meanings beyond the quick recognition-meanings developed in the interactive area. *We shall therefore use the search for meanings, of the deeper sort, as a second indicator of inmost-self activity.*

Third, in the inmost self, if anywhere, one would expect to find a source for those useful and novel ideas that are not generated in our conscious experiencing self, nor by chance, but that seem to pop into consciousness from some hidden inspiration. Such ideas are not plausibly assignable to brain action. The ordinary, the usual, the habitual, the reflexive, the instinctive, are all arguably handled in the brain or the inter-

active area. But the life-meaning of a novel idea—and, therefore, its use to us—cannot be measured by intensities of
stimuli of the sort that control neuronal action. As Straus
remarks, "A slight variation of tone and gesture may make us
feel thunderstruck, like Falstaff facing Prince Henry, his
'King Hal,' after the coronation"—this slight shift revealing
to Falstaff a wholly altered relationship.[2] So, too, with a new
theoretical idea; its power bears no relation to the intensity of
the sense stimuli that either precede or follow it. Chance, as
we shall see, can usually be ruled out as a sufficient explanation for the evocation of such an idea. Thus the experiencing
of a useful and novel idea will suggest that we look to the inmost self for those associations or combinations that evoked
it. However, we shall not take a single one of these criteria,
but all three of them together, as plausible evidence for the
generating of an experience out of inmost-self activity. *The
test for inmost-self activity, then, will be that one experiences
an idea or act, emerging from the unconscious, which is novel, useful, deeply meaningful and drawing on pure memories.*

We cannot hope to separate out with certainty what is solely superconscious inmost-self activity from activity influenced
by the subconscious interactive area. If my view is correct
about movements in the self, as set forth in Chapter Ten, we
can learn of inmost-self activity only when it leads us to act
overtly or to have a conscious inward experience—and such
actions and experiences are all mediated normally through the
interactive area. However, the three criteria chosen do seem
to fit the inmost self rather than the interactive area. The
interactive area, as we have seen, transmits and translates our
perceptual, affective and motoric activity. On its own it may
generate some novel experiences (from drug-induced or
chance firings or neuron systems), but those experiences will
not often be useful, while the useful experiences arising from
the interactive area alone are not often novel ones. The interactive area, instead of the novel, operates normally with the
habitual, the skilled, the structured: and these schemata are
its memory, while the pure memory of individual events
dwells in the inmost self. As for motives, the interactive area

seems to be swayed by hedonic charges rather than by a broad thirst for meanings. For these reasons it seems unlikely (at least moderately implausible) that the interactive area, on its own, originates many actions or conscious experiences that are useful, novel, pure-memory-based and broadly meaning-oriented.

We shall therefore explore several great powers of the mind—intellect, imagination, will, and judgment—with a rather narrow focus.* That is, we shall seek examples of conscious experiences based on unconscious operations that draw upon *pure memories,* that *seek meanings* and that help generate *useful and novel ideas.* These examples will plausibly illustrate what kind of activities occur in the superconscious inmost self as it cooperates with the conscious experiencing self. It should be stressed that these are, in fact, only examples, used as illustrations. They are not attempts to map the full scope or nature of these powers of the mind. What we seek here is not a comprehensive philosophical anthropology. *We seek rather sufficient illustrations of superconscious inmost-self activity to establish what kinds of operations, if any, go on there, outside the brain.* If this can be positively established, we shall be a further long step ahead toward meaningful survival after death—a survival embracing not only the self's pure memories but also major mental activities. We begin with intellective thinking.

---

*I use *mind,* in humans, to mean the active organizing principle in the soul. I use *soul* to mean the "who" of the self, that is, the I and its intentional field (that field extending over the contents of the inmost and experiencing self, into the interactive area and perhaps beyond).

15

The Inmost Self–
Thinking

Intellective thinking is a relating of two or more mental objects, aimed at knowledge.* This occurs whenever we reflect. It happens as I puzzle out what I did with the theater tickets I bought three weeks ago, which are now unaccountably lost. It happens as I read along in a mystery and try to confirm my hunch that the sexy sister-in-law is really the murderer. It can happen even in checking out what's wrong with a motorcycle, as Robert Pirsig wittily shows in his novel on Zen and the art of motorcycle maintenance.[1] But the most striking examples of intellection—and the deepest involvement of the inmost self—occur in creative thinking. Here we find in superlative degree a thinking that is useful, novel, drawing on pure memories, and broadly meaning-oriented. These are our indicators of inmost-self activity. So we shall focus now on the area of creative thought.

---

*By *mental object* I mean anything that can be directly experienced as a single entity. Such an object may not currently appear in the conscious experiencing self; it may exist in the superconscious or subconscious, but it must be capable of entering consciousness without transformation.

The reader will note that I have separated intellective thinking from judgment, which is treated in Chapter Eighteen. Judgment is traditionally a power of "the intellect," considered as a mental faculty. I wish to avoid the faculty approach. I would encourage the reader to think of active powers or functioning of the inmost self, not faculties.

Four usual stages have been distinguished in creative thinking. First comes a *preparative* period of investigating a problem deeply without finding a solution. In the second or *incubation* period the troubled thinker puts the problem out of his consciousness. Third, *illumination* arrives, a sudden insight, a revelation of the answer. Lastly, a stage of *verification* is needed.[2]

What concerns us here particularly is the incubation stage leading up to illumination. This incubation seems to occur mostly in the inmost self. Often it involves a linking of elements from two very different contexts of experience. One of these contexts may be current while the other dwells deep in the pure memory store. The history of science and technology offers many examples, as Arthur Koestler points out.

Thus Johannes Gutenberg, seeking a practical method of printing large sheets of paper, found himself stumped. Playing-cards at that time were imprinted by a rubbing method, but this only smudged the small letters Gutenberg was using. Wherever he went he carried with him, in his inmost self, this incubating problem of how to print large sheets. His inspiration came, as he wrote, when "I took part in the wine harvest. I watched the wine flowing, and going back from the effect to the cause, I studied the power of this press which nothing can resist." Then came the "ray of light": and from a linking of his own problem with the wine press, Gutenberg developed the printing press.[3]

A notable American example of creative incubation came from Benjamin Franklin. Experimenting with electricity, Franklin speculated that lightning is in fact an electrical discharge. But how could lightning be brought safely to earth, to find out? At some moment, dipping deep into pure memory, Franklin recalled his childhood sport of kite flying. He linked this with the lightning problem. With his young son he rigged up a kite and drained some of a storm cloud's charge into a Leyden jar, where it did indeed behave like electricity. Later Franklin put the discovery to practical use by rigging up lightning rods for homes.

Another case of old pure memories in the inmost self leading to new insight occurred with Alfred Russel Wallace.

Wallace, an English naturalist, developed the same theory of evolution through natural selection that Charles Darwin did, at much the same time; and the two men collaborated on the first great paper about it, in 1848. Both men puzzled long, and separately, over what could impel the evolution of species. An illuminative insight came to Wallace, as he later wrote, one night on an island near New Guinea where he lay "muffled in blankets in the cold fit of a severe attack of intermittent fever." He suddenly recalled a book he had read twelve or more years earlier. The book was Malthus's essay on population, predicting ever greater pressure on the world's scarce resources from a rising human population.

"It suddenly flashed upon me," Wallace wrote, "that this self-action process (that is, the struggle for existence) would *necessarily improve the race,* because in every generation the inferior would inevitably be killed off and the superior would remain—that is, *the fittest would survive."* Thinking it over, he became convinced that "I had at length found the long-sought-for law of nature that solved the problem of the origin of the species." Whatever one may think of Wallace's answer, we note that this problem had been incubating in him for several years, awaiting a creative linkage with pure memories dating back at least twelve years. His insight thus meets our criteria for inmost self activity, being a useful and novel idea drawing on long-term pure memories in response to Wallace's search for meanings.

Again, one afternoon in 1865, a chemistry professor in Ghent, F. A. von Kekulé, was dozing by the fire. He had been fruitlessly seeking the structure of an important class of organic compounds. Now he fell into a dream or perhaps a daydream. The atoms, as he later wrote, seemed to gambol before his eyes. They formed into long rows. They twined and twisted like snakes. Then, of a sudden, "one of the snakes had seized hold of its own tail, and the form whirled mockingly before my eyes. As if by a flash of lightning I awoke . . . " And with this insight, this linkage of his incubating problem with a snake swallowing its tail, Kekulé grasped the ringlike structure of the benzene molecule, an epochal discovery in organic chemistry: a further example of the superconscious inmost self in creative activity.

Kekulé's account makes one think of another remarkable achievement nearly ninety years later, when the double helix structure of DNA molecules was revealed by Francis Crick and James Watson. But that discovery resulted not from one happy hit but from a long alternation of hunch-test-hunch-test-hunch-test. That, too, is a frequent pattern in scientific thought.[4]

Another example of creativity during sleep—and the use of long-buried pure memories—occurred to the physiologist Otto Loewi. In 1903 Loewi suggested to a friend that a chemical agent may be involved when a nerve terminal activates a muscle or gland, but he saw no way to test it. Fifteen years later Loewi designed an experiment that kept frogs' hearts beating in a salt solution. Two years after that, in the middle of the night, the long hidden incubation in Loewi's inmost self reached an end. As he later recalled, he awoke, turned on the light, and jotted down a few notes on a tiny slip of paper. Then he fell asleep again. "It occurred to me at six o'clock in the morning that during the night I had written down something most important, but I was unable to decipher the scrawl." Fortunately, the next night at 3:00 a.m. the same idea returned. "It was the design of an experiment," he reported, "to determine whether or not the hypothesis of chemical transmission that I had uttered seventeen years ago was correct." Loewi got up immediately, went to his laboratory, and "performed the simple experiment on a frog heart according to the nocturnal design." This experiment won Loewi the Nobel Prize. In his own words: "The story of this discovery shows that an idea may sleep for decades in the unconscious mind and then suddenly return." Here, too, we observe creative activity in the inmost self.

Another outstanding physiologist, Walter Cannon, has also testified to the creativity of night-wakefulness, when ideas emerge from the "extra-conscious." In one such "illuminating moment," he wrote, he invented a complex new laboratory device, which was "presented to me as a complete mechanism in a brief period of insight when I awoke in the night.'' Another time, Cannon found a meaningful explanation for the diverse and seemingly unrelated bodily changes that occur in great emotional excitement such as fear and rage. "One wakeful night," he wrote, "after a considerable collection of these changes had been disclosed, the idea flashed through my mind that they could be nicely integrated if conceived as bodily preparations for supreme effort in flight or in fighting." Further investigation "confirmed the general scheme suggested by the hunch."[5]

Mathematicians, the most abstract of creative thinkers, also testify to inspiration in the inmost self, out of all conscious awareness. The French mathematician Henri Poincaré has given a remarkable account of how he came upon one of his greatest discoveries, Fuchsian functions. By day, working hard at his desk, he made no progress. But during a sleepless night, while ideas rose in crowds in his mind and he "felt them collide," he gained his first insights. Other crucial insights came when he was consciously occupied at completely other tasks: while putting his foot on the step to enter a bus, while walking on a bluff at the seaside, and while away on his military service. Poincaré concluded that the unconscious self "is in no way inferior to the conscious self; it is not merely automatic; it is capable of discernment; it has tact, delicacy; it knows how to choose, to divine."[6] These attributes seem to apply much more plausibly to the superconscious inmost self, as it draws on our pure memories, than they apply to any kind of neurological arrangement.

Jacques Hadamard, another French mathematician, makes a further point about creative intellection. Earlier conscious efforts, he notes, are "really work," but the illuminating insight comes into awareness suddenly, without any preceptible effort. In his own case, Hadamard recalls: "On being very abruptly awakened by an external noise, a (mathematical) solution long searched for appeared to me at once without the slightest instant of reflection on my part . . . and in a quite different direction from any of those which I had previously tried to follow."[7] Clearly this solution had incubated in his inmost self while he slept.

Most curious of all are those thinkers who draw not only on pure memory and the usual kinds of creative linkage but on some deep inmost vision, ahead of their times. Hadamard cites two such examples. Girolamo Cardan (1501-1576), an Italian mathematician, physician and writer, not only invented a gear-joint later used in automobiles but also fundamentally changed mathematics by the invention of imaginaries. An imaginary, Hadamard points out, is a quantity that is a mathematical absurdity, for example, the square root of a negative number. Cardan deliberately committed that absurdity and began to calculate on such imaginary quantities. "One would describe this," says Hadamard, "as pure madness; and yet the whole (later) development of algebra and analysis would have been impossible without that fundament."

Evariste Galois, another mathematician, died in a duel in 1832 at the age of twenty. Galois, writes Hadamard, spent the night before the duel revising his notes on his discoveries. Seeming to foresee his death, he worked on a manuscript the Academy of Sciences had rejected and also wrote to a friend "scanty and hurried mention of other beautiful views." Galois' profound ideas, reports Hadamard, were at first forgotten and only later drew attention. The rejected manuscript was found to signify "a total transformation of higher algebra," while another theorem of Galois gained importance and meaning only through mathematical discoveries made after his death.

All these examples illustrate a high use of creative intellect. They reveal a power of thinking that is novel (sometimes revolutionary), useful (sometimes only generations later), drawing on pure memories (some of them many years old), and oriented to a deep meaning, a divining and unlocking of nature's mysteries. They illustrate the superconscious inmost self in action, based on the criteria for such activity. Few among us can equal such insights. But each of us possesses an inmost self. Each of us does some intellective thinking and gains some insights. Each of us uses his or her own superconscious as much more than a memory store. Therefore, if our superconscious self survives death, what survives may plausibly be more than mere memories. It may well include creative insights building on what we have remembered from our present life but reaching beyond that, into new creativity.

16

The Inmost Self–Imagining

Imagining is a relating of two or more mental objects, aimed usually at a new creation. The "usually" is inserted because some images seem to arise more from accident than from any intention (though one's mind may interpret or develop them meaningfully after they do arise). These accidental images include many hallucinatory events caused by abnormal brain functioning, induced by drugs, alcohol, disease, or various kinds of withdrawal.

The usual imaginary event-series, though, does have an aim: to make something new. On the way toward this, according to our model of the self, the inmost self reassembles chunks of pure memories into new relationships, as we shall see. This assemblage slips through the subconscious, sometimes with much distortion, and then into consciousness. The conscious imaginary presentation evokes a further assemblage in the inmost self, and the process continues.

Imagination displays itself most notably as daydreams, rehearsings, creative imaginings, hallucinations, delusions, dreams, and dreamy states.[1] I shall not deal here with hallucinations, delusions, dreams, and dreamy states (that is, states between waking and sleeping). With these, the influences of brain-tied schemata and of the inmost self are too complexly intertwined. Instead, I shall cite some examples of the other types of imagination that seem plausibly to originate in the superconscious inmost self.

Daydreams have been studied in depth by Jerome L. Singer, a psychologist.[2] His own daydreams, Singer reports, have been of two quite different types. Most consist of his on-going stream of consciousness, private interior monologues, and at times somewhat more organized fantasies. But "the main feature of my own mental life in childhood and adolescence," he writes, consisted of "a series of recurring fairly elaborate fantasies," involving heroic adventures.

One of these was the "Poppy Ott, Football Hero" fantasy. This grew out of a series of boys' books, one of whose characters, Poppy Ott, Singer took over and developed through a long series of imaginative football games. Singer also evolved a "Great Statesman" fantasy. This featured a noble but nameless senator. In fantasied incident after incident, Singer reports, Senator X shone forth as "a great moral figure in American life, a foe of corruption or blind conservatism, defender of the republic, a towering individual in the service of his people." Singer notes the soap opera quality of this fantasy, but it "did not seem at all banal to me" from ages eleven to eighteen.

A further example was "Singer the Great Composer." This, Singer says, grew out of his crude attempts to play the piano at age ten, when "I began substituting inner harmony for the rather mediocre external efforts I was producing." This fantasy activity, Singer reports, "has never really stopped," but Singer the Great Composer has "faded to a pale shadow of the richness and excitement it had for me in early adolescence."

These extended fantasies may remind the reader of his or her own adolescent daydreams—or perhaps some current ones. Nearly all of us, according to surveys, continue to daydream into adulthood. Most of our fantasies are far less elaborate than Singer's. They may range from practical anticipations to castles-in-Spain wish fulfillment, with imaginings of sexual adventure, revenge, or luxurious living. Clearly the impetus behind a daydream often stems from our subconscious hedonic level. But Singer's book-length study makes plain that the daydreaming process draws on chunks of pure memory to form novel and useful mental structures, seeking to add meaning to one's life. These are the three key indicators of inmost self activity. Daydreams thus offer an important example of activity originating in the inmost self.

Rehearsings are included by Singer in his practical daydreaming, but they seem worthy of a separate category. Rehearsings are what we do when we plan for a future event or project, by way of imagery. That is, we picture to ourself just how it will happen. Building on chunks of past memory, we recombine and project a new future. We may even give the future event alternative scenarios, depending on what some other participant does, what the weather is like, whether we get the raise we expect, and so on. Some people, including the writer, do this sort of imaginary rehearsing quite often, applying it to a wide range of future activities—anything from the plan for Saturday morning's shopping to a project for buying a cottage somewhere along the Mediterranean. Here, too, we find the three indicators of inmost self activity: recombining pure memories in a novel and useful way, in search of meaning.

Creative imagining denotes the mental aspect of creating new works of art. The poet and critic Brewster Ghiselin has assembled an intriguing set of first-hand accounts of this.[3] These deal with the various fine arts, but a similar process operates no doubt in the practical arts. The creator's inspiration seems to incubate from one or more seeds falling in well-cultivated soil. These then sprout and bud and intermingle in the pure-memory seedbed of his or her inmost self, emerging later into conscious bloom. Thus Wordsworth's famed remark that poetry "takes its origin from emotion recollected in tranquility." His recollected emotion must have emerged from the pure memory store of his inmost self. Some examples:

The poet A. E. Housman tells of composing while on afternoon walks, after drinking a pint of beer at lunch. He would wander along, thinking of nothing in particular, when "there would flow into my mind, with sudden and unaccountable emotion, sometimes a line or two of verse, sometimes a whole stanza at once, accompanied, not preceded, by a vague notion of the poem which they were destined to form a part of.'' Then he would encounter a lull of an hour or so, whereupon ''perhaps the spring would bubble up again.'' Otherwise, ''the poem had to be taken in hand and completed by the brain, which was apt to be a matter of trouble and anxiety, involving trial and disappointment, and sometimes ending in failure.''

Stephen Spender writes that ''memory exercised in a particular way is the natural gift of poetic genius.'' The poet, above all else, he declares, is someone ''who never forgets certain sense-impressions which he has experienced and which he can re-live again and again as though in all their original freshness.'' In his own case, Spender cites ''overwhelming'' associations which, suddenly aroused, ''have carried me back so completely into the past, particularly into my own childhood, that I have lost all sense of the present time and place.''

Katherine Anne Porter has observed, about her way of composing a story, that she ''must very often refer far back in time to seek the meaning or explanation of today's smallest event, and I have long since lost the power to be astonished at what I find there.'' Speaking of her ''constant exercises of memory,'' she reflects that ''all my experience seems to be simply memory, with continuity, marginal notes, constant revision and comparison of one thing with another.'' At times, a host of memories ''converge, harmonize, arrange themselves around a central idea in a coherent form, and I write a story.''

Friedrich Nietzsche, describing the composition of *Thus Spake Zarathustra,* wrote: ''One hears—one does not seek; one takes—one does not ask who gives: a thought flashes out like lightning, inevitably without hesitation—I have never had any choice about it.''

In painting, Picasso has been quoted by Christian Zervos as saying: ''How would you have a spectator live my picture as I have lived it? A picture comes to me from far off, who knows how far, I divined it, I saw it, I made it, and yet next day I myself don't see what I have done." In contrast Henry Moore stresses the need for conscious control and organization as well as nonconscious inspiration in art. A sculptor especially, he writes, "must strive continually to think of and use form in its full spatial completeness." The sculptor "gets the solid shape, as it were, inside his head." He mentally visualizes "a complex form *from all round itself:* he knows while he looks at one side what the other side is like; he identifies himself with its centre of gravity, its mass, its weight; he realizes its volume, as the space that the shape displaces in the air."

As for music, a letter ascribed to Mozart gives this account of his inspirations:

> When I feel well and in a good humor, or when I am taking a drive or walking after a good meal, or in the night when I cannot sleep, (musical) thoughts crowd into my mind as easily as you could wish. Whence and how do they come? I do not know and I have nothing to do with it. Those which please me, I keep in my head and hum them; at least others have told me that I do so. Once I have my theme, another melody comes, linking itself to the first one, in accordance with the needs of the composition as a whole: the counterpoint, the part of each instrument, and all these melodic fragments at last produce the entire work. Then my soul is on fire with inspiration, if however nothing occurs to distract my attention. The work grows; I keep expanding it, conceiving it more and more clearly until I have the entire composition finished in my head though it may be long. Then my mind seizes it as a glance of my eye a beautiful picture or a handsome youth. It does not come to me successively, with its various parts worked out in detail, as they will be later on, but it is in its entirety that my imagination lets me hear it.[4]

What is most striking about these accounts of creative inspiration is the expansion or spreading out of consciousness. It is as though the veil had almost vanished between the conscious mind and portions of the superconscious, as though the full mind were almost united in a certain area of its spread-out reality. This almost-union, as Spender noted, may pull the creator away from his present physical environment. He may become abstracted. He may feel a peculiar excitement, evoked at his hedonic level by this unusual mind state. Not for nothing did Plato suggest that poets are "bereft of their senses" by their god-given inspirations.

As natural events, however, we can plausibly class creative imaginings along with rehearsings and daydreams. All are states of mind that draw on pure memories to create, out of the unconscious, something meaningful, new, and useful. These are the criteria we have established for inmost self activity. Thus these examples of imagining are also illustrations of what goes on in the superconscious nonorganic part of us. They open a further possibility that any survival after death will be active and creative, not merely passive.

As to the significance of the artist's imaginative vision, no one has spoken more eloquently than William Blake:

> To the eye of a miser a guinea is far more beautiful than the sun and a bag worn with the use of money has more beautiful proportions than a vine filled with grapes. The tree which moves some to tears of joy is in the eyes of others only a green thing which stands in the way. As a man is, so he sees.
>
> When the sun rises, do you not see a round disk of fire something like a gold piece? O no, no, I see an innumerable company of the Heavenly host crying 'Holy, Holy, Holy, is the Lord God Almighty.' I do not question my bodily eye any more than I would question a window concerning sight. I look through it and not with it.[5]

17

The Inmost Self–Willing

Willing is the coupling of one or more mental objects with assent, aimed at achievement. Thus willing is future oriented. It ranges over an immense variety of activities, from the most trivial decisions (Shall I take this bus or the next one, which may be less crowded?) to the most momentous life choices (Shall I become a doctor? Shall I marry her? Shall I accept the Christian faith?). Willing implies a voluntary act. Thus behavior impelled by purely organic causes (at the somatic or hedonic level only) would not be a willed act. Willing, therefore, is noetic, an act of the subjective I. But it need not be wholly conscious. The coupling of a mental object with assent may brush as lightly across one's consciousness as a wisp of smoke. One may not be really aware of the decision. And yet, if one's I has imagined an object or activity, and assented, then one has willed the act. When I pop the forbidden chocolate in my mouth, it is a voluntary deed.

We cannot here deal in depth with either the philosophy or psychology of will. Our aim is simply to illustrate the role of willing in the superconscious self. However, a few general comments will be useful before we turn to some examples of the kind of willing plausibly generated in the inmost self.

What one's willing aims to achieve is a new state of affairs involving the assented-to mental object or objects, to be reached through one's own activity or, in some cases, through refraining from activity. By *assent* here is meant a "yes" attitude. This attitude may range into an intense feeling of love and yearning; but the only assent that needs to occur is simply that the mental object(s) are now held in awareness, or summoned back to awareness, without being shoved away by some alternate or opposing mental object(s).

The aim at achievement implies that willing is goal directed. The goal may be an end in itself, or it may be a subordinate or instrumental goal, i.e., a task, directed to an end beyond itself. The aim at achievement—the thrust toward action—distinguishes willing from wishing. One may wish, in daydreams or fantasies, for all kinds of delicious or vengeful scenarios; but one is not then aiming at achievement. However, such an aim does not imply that one seeks only what can be got. People may aim at, and will, a goal beyond their powers.

As for how the will works, let us turn to William James's classical discussion.[1] Here is one example he gives, a familiar one no doubt to his nineteenth-century readers:

> We know what it is to get out of bed on a freeezing morning in a room without a fire, and how the very vital principle within us protests against the ordeal. Probably most persons have lain on certain mornings for an hour at a time unable to brace themselves to the resolve. We think how late we shall be, how the duties of the day will suffer; we say, "I *must* get up, this is ignominious," etc.; but still the warm couch feels too delicious, the cold outside too cruel, and resolution faints away and postpones itself again and again just as it seemed on the verge of bursting the resistance and passing over into the decisive act. Now how do we ever get up under such circumstances? If I may generalize from my own experience, we more often than not get up without any struggle or decision at all. We suddenly find that we *have* got up. A fortunate lapse of consciousness occurs; we forget both the warmth and the cold; we fall into some revery connected with the day's life, in the course of which the idea flashes across us, "Hollo! I must lie here no longer"—an idea which at that lucky instant awakens no contradictory or paralyzing suggestions, and consequently produces immediately its appropriate motor effects. It was our

acute consciousness of both the warmth and the cold during the period of struggle, which paralyzed our activity then and kept our idea of rising in the condition of *wish* and not of *will*. The moment these inhibitory ideas ceased, the original idea exerted its effects. This case seems to me to contain in miniature form the data for an entire psychology of volition.

Thus James suggests that the crucial element in effective willing is a sustained imagined idea (our "mental object") of the activity or results desired. This may be blocked by inhibitory ideas; but as soon as those can be dissipated, the forward movement proceeds. At times however, James adds, a *fiat* or resolve comes in. At times one may engage in long deliberation. At times a fierce mental struggle may ensue. But the core of the whole affair is whether one can hold before one's awareness the willed idea or some token of it. This is true not merely for casual matters but for the most serious life choices, James affirms. "The deepest question that is ever asked," he writes, "admits of no reply" but a resolute "turning of the will."[2]

Indeed these kinds of life turning-points are better examples for our purpose than the ordinary daily exercise of willing. That is, these resolves—the touchstone choices and beliefs that change the motion of a whole life—seem most plausibly generated and lodged in the inmost self, while the daily decisions may be more heavily influenced by subconscious schemata. These central resolves quintessentially carry our search for meanings, draw on past pure memories, and seek to remold the world (or a small part of it) in useful and novel ways. They thus exemplify the criteria for activity in the inmost self. Psychologist Gordon Allport calls this central willing by the name of "propriate striving," and he notes that "the characteristic feature of such striving is its resistance to equilibrium: tension is maintained rather than reduced."[3] As an example, Allport recalls that the young Roald Amundsen from the age of fifteen, in 1887, had one dominant passion—to become a polar explorer. The obstacles seemed insurmountable, and they continued throughout Amundsen's life. But despite all the tensions, the Norwegian refused to yield in his propriate striving. Each success only raised the level of his aspiration. First he sailed the Northwest Passage. Then he led the "painful project" that discovered the South Pole in 1911. For years thereafter, with little money and great discouragements, Amundsen planned to fly over the North Pole, a task finally achieved. In the end, aged fifty-six, he again ventured into the Arctic to rescue another explorer, Nobile—and lost his own life. Allport, as a psychologist, concludes:

> Propriate striving distinguishes itself from other forms of motivation in that, however beset by conflicts, it makes for unification of personality . . . . The possession of long-range goals, regarded as central to one's personal existence, distinguishes the human being from the animal, the adult from the child, and in many cases the healthy personality from the sick.

In this central willing, each of us chooses his or her own life goal. What we choose may derive from the kind of extended adolescent daydreaming described by Singer in the last chapter. Or it may be fixed by a living person as model, or by a single "vision" of some kind—artistic, religious, metaphysical. Sir John Eccles, a Nobel Prize winning neurophysiologist, has described his own driving vision as focussed on the question of what is the nature of man's "conscious experiencing self" and its unique relation to a particular brain. "To me," he writes, "they are the most fundamental and important questions that can be asked," and he adds that he has "held this belief since I was eighteen years old, when I had a kind of sudden illumination of these problems, and I have been driven on by their interest and urgency to spend my life studying the nervous system."[4]

Likewise the Austrian physicist Ernst Mach describes an early metaphysical illumination that focussed his lifelong strivings. This happened, he writes, some two or three years after he had read Immanuel Kant, at the age of fifteen. In an abrupt insight, he threw over Kant's philosophy in favor of a complete empiricism. "On a bright summer day in the open air," Mach writes, "the world with my ego suddenly appeared to me as *one* coherent mass of sensations, only more strongly coherent in the ego." This moment, he writes, "was decisive for my whole view," and he spent a lifetime of scientific work seeking to establish it.[5] But for each person who commits himself for such an intellectual goal, ten probably commit themselves for power, a score for money, a hundred for love.

Since this kind of central willing usually leads into effort or struggle, it is important that we distinguish the execution of the willing from the act of willing. The act of willing, as James pointed out, is simply bringing a certain idea (mental object) before our awareness, coupled with assent. No physical effort is involved here. Rather, it is the execution of the act, the seeking of the goal, that plunges us into somatic and hedonic effort. However, at the noetic level, rival ideas may try to displace the willed idea or its token. Hedonic-somatic demands may batter at the willed idea on its way from superconscious into consciousness. Or they may idealize themselves into an enticing or despairing scenario, and with this may try to whip the willed idea from our conscious mind.

An example from my own life might clarify this. Some years ago I gave up smoking. I found it immensely hard to do. I had tried twice before to quit cigarettes and failed. I knew all the well-publicized facts about smoking and health, but my addiction ruled me; it kept prompting my mind to make excuses. Then a colleague in the office next to mine came down with lung cancer. One of his lungs was removed. Some months later he returned to work a few hours a day. He was grey and gaunt; his mustache had turned white; he would cough in spasms into his handkerchief and then slowly curse. He still smoked his favorite cigarettes. "Why stop now?" he said. I told myself: "You must decide. Do you want to die in agony ten years from now, like Ed, or do you want to live a normal lifetime?" I also told myself: "If you stop now, and then go back to smoking, it means you have no will whatever, you will never achieve what you want in life, you will amount to nothing at all." From that moment I stopped, some weeks before Ed died. Withdrawal symptoms assailed me for months. They came in several ways. Flashing through my mind would go the old habit-sequence: cigarette pack up from my pocket, jump one out, tap it, into mouth, light it: all ready to go, needing only assent. Or: "Gee, cigarette . . . good . . . now," with a panting openness of trachea and throat. Or: the smell of someone smoking, "Ah . . . *yes,*" and imagined feel of lit cigarette between my fingers, lifting to my lips, sucking pleasurably in. To banish these mental objects, these triggers to action and downfall, I had only certain other mental objects: an image of Ed's gaunt face, a verbal phrase that reduced itself to "want to die?" and another phrase that shrank simply to "no will." With those three little token mental objects I broke the habit and whipped my body's addiction. To achieve this cost me months of inner struggle. But (our key point here) my act of willing and sustaining my will involved only bringing certain mental objects before my consciousness and rejecting others.

We must not conclude, though, that central noetic willing and the somatic-hedonic levels are necessarily opposed. On the contrary. As the psychologist Rollo May points out, fruitful use of will often involves "a listening to the body." He recounts a striking example from his own life. Many years ago he was hospitalized with tuberculosis. At that time the only cure for TB was bed rest and carefully graduated exercise. May found that exerting "will power" to get well did him no good at all, and that "the 'strong-willed' dominating type of person with TB generally got worse." Rather, he writes, "when I could be sensitive to my body, 'hear' that I was fatigued and needed to rest more, or sense that my body was strong enough for me to increase my exercise, I got better. When I found awareness of my body blocked off . . . I got worse." By this "listening" to the body, May suggests, both he and other patients helped cure themselves of the often-fatal disease.[6]

Central willing may be used not only to sustain oneself but also to achieve, to build, to create—a garden or a palace, a business enterprise or a work of art, a social reform or a loving family or a soaring dam. Or one's central will may bid one simply to serve those in need. No doubt the reader knows at least one person whose life shines with such service. Countless examples could be used to illustrate this point. We shall pluck two of them from history, to mark a central willing that serves.

Joseph Damien de Veuster, a Belgian priest, sailed as a missionary to the Hawaiian Islands in 1864 at the age of twenty-four. The colony of lepers on the island of Molokai had no pastor, and in 1873 Father Damien volunteered to his bishop to go and serve them. That same day, without any farewells, he sailed with the bishop on a boat taking some fifty lepers to Molokai. On arrival, the bishop assembled the lepers and told them this new priest "does not hesitate to become one of you, to live and die with you." Then the bishop left.

Father Damien had no doubt of his fate, but he worked with good cheer for ten years before it befell him. He then wrote to the bishop: "I cannot come to Honolulu, for leprosy has attacked me. There are signs of it on my left cheek and ear and my eyebrows are beginning to fall, I shall soon be quite disfigured . . . ." After that, in preaching, Damien no longer said "my brethren" but "we lepers." As Quiller-Couch recounts, he went steadily forward to the end, instructing his fellow outcasts, receiving their confessions, binding their sores, even feeding them, putting their food into their mouths when the leprosy had eaten away their hands—all the while facing the sight of what lay ahead for him as well. When death came, his friends buried Damien under the pandanus tree whose boughs had been his roof when he first came to Molokai.[7]

In our own century, consider the life of a Russian woman named Elizabeth Pilenko. She came from a wealthy land-owning family and attended the university in St. Petersburg. As a young woman she published two books of poems, made friends with other Petersburg poets, and also taught evening classes at the great Putilov factory. She became a socialist revolutionary agitator in the years before the Bolshevik revolution of 1917. She was mayor of her home town in southern Russia during the civil war between Whites and Reds, trying to gain justice for the townsfolk from both sides. In 1923, despairing of the revolution's excesses, she fled to France. There she turned from Marx to religion. She presented herself to leaders of the Russian Church in Paris, saying she wished to become a nun and to found a convent, "beginning at once, today." She had her way, but it was not the usual way. Early each morning she would be at the markets, buying cheap food for the people she fed, carrying it home in a sack on her back. With her worn black habit and ancient men's shoes, Mother Maria (as she was then known) became a familiar figure in the Paris slums. She served mostly the Russian refugees, many of them desperately poor. She discovered a group of them with tuberculosis, living in a hovel. Still the agitator, she started out with ten francs in her pocket, bought a chateau, and opened a sanatorium. She raised another outcry and got many Russian refugees released from mental institutions, where they had been locked up by local authorities simply to get rid of them.

When the Nazis occupied France in World War II, Mother Maria felt she must devote herself to saving persecuted Jews. She and her chaplain made the convent a haven for Jews and several hundred were helped to escape. At the end of a month the Gestapo came. The chaplain was sent to Buchenwald camp, where he died of starvation. Mother Maria was sent to Ravensbruck camp. As recounted by others soon after the war, this is what happened to her: She had been at Ravensbruck two and a half years, winning respect even from the guards, when a new block of buildings went up. These were gas chambers. The inmates were told they were hot baths. On a certain day several dozen women were lined up outside the buildings. One girl became hysterical. Mother Maria, who had not been selected, gently told the girl: "Don't be frightened. Look, I shall take your turn." She stood in line with the rest and passed through the doors. This was on Good Friday, 1945.[8]

Father Damien and Elizabeth Pilenko both lived lives marked by a central willing to serve.[9] They freely choose this course of life. Often they must have been tempted to change course. At times, no doubt, they fell away from their directedness; but always they came back to it. In each of them this central willing, once chosen by the subjective I, organized the subjective I. This willing guided the actions, feelings, and thoughts that made of the inward person what that person became; it integrated the meaning of that person's life. And since, as we earlier saw, the subjective I and its thirst for meaning are located in the inmost self, this kind of central willing most plausibly originates in the inmost self. That means the organizing, integrating power over the self displayed in central willing may be available to us after death, if the inmost self survives the mortal organism.

18

The Inmost Self– Judging

Judging is the relating of one or more mental objects and a larger context, aimed at harmony. This definition is very broad, but so are the varieties of judgment. Judging ranges from picking out a necktie to the elaborate legal balancing of facts and conclusions by a Supreme Court justice. All the mental activities cited earlier—intellective, imaginative and willed—nearly always include elements of judging. Indeed one might call judgment the keystone of the arch of human be-ing. The other stones of the arch—not only perception, memory, intellect, imagination and will, but also our organic drives, our emotions, feelings, and desires—all these are crucial to making us what we are. But the keystone of judgment holds us together. Without a proper keystone—good judgment—our be-ing loses its rightful meaning. Lacking judgment, our life becomes distorted, skewed, anomalous, and may even collapse. We shall dip into history for an illustration.

Benjamin Rush (1745-1813) was not only the most renowned American physician of his day but also a man of noble spirit. He served in the Continental Congress, signed the Declaration of Independence, was cofounder of our first antislavery society, cofounder and professor at the Pennsylvania Medical College. When an epidemic of yellow fever hit the nation's capital, Philadelphia, in the summer of 1793, much of the government fled, and so did half of the city's 55,000 people. Dr. Rush stayed. All through that summer and fall, while 5,000 Philadelphians died, Dr. Rush gave of himself. He saw and treated a hundred, then a hundred and twenty patients a day. By mid-September, as he wrote his wife, he was sleeping only three or four hours a night. Then he himself fell ill. Shock ran through the city. But Dr. Rush rallied. He rose from his sick bed, began prescribing in his parlor, and even resumed his visiting of the sick. His fever persisted. He had trouble climbing stairs. The stench of the sickrooms made him dizzy. Still he continued, treating as many as a hundred and fifty a day. He prayed continually, and begged others to pray for Philadelphia. As historian J. M. Powell recounts, "Responding to his courage, inspired by his abundant vitality, his kindness and optimism, elevated by his evocative faith, people adored Dr. Rush." And yet, as Powell observes, Rush's prescriptions against yellow fever—the mercury purge and copious bloodletting—were "erroneous, and probably fatal, treatments." Other physicians insisted on this fact. Rush could not see it. He felt sure he knew best. "He was wrong," Powell writes, "tragically, disastrously, frightfully wrong . . . nor shall we ever know how many lives his errors cost." In this crisis, the man lacked judgment.[1]

What are the standards for good judgment? Immanuel Kant proposed that judgment means subsuming a particular under some universal rule or law.[2] But this seems only partly correct. In some areas, for example, logic and morals, certain principles are almost universal. In other areas, for example aesthetics, diversity of opinion seems widespread. Thus one can say of judging only that it employs a larger context, and not necessarily a universal rule or law. Does judging always call on the superconscious inmost self? Here again, one must say that it does not. Many judgments of a routine kind, such as picking out a quarter, a dime, and a nickel to pay for a forty-cent newspaper, are evidently made through the subconscious schemata of the interactive area, closely tied to brain activity. In this chapter, though, we shall touch on a few examples where the "larger context" that is used seems to require more than brain activity as a source. In these examples one can plausibly deduce an involvement of the inmost self. These judgments use pure memories in novel ways in search of meaningful goals; and those are the criteria we set in Chapter Fourteen as indicators of inmost self activity.

We shall briefly consider five kinds of judgment. Each of these operates with different sorts of contexts. Sometimes, of course, one combines two or more types of judgment. The five types are: practical, logical, moral, aesthetic, and cosmic. In *practical judgment* one seeks to harmonize a mental object or objects with relevant aspects of the real world. By real world, in this case, is meant the world we have to live in —physical, social, and personal. The type of harmony sought here is usually truth as a basis for action. Take as an example the judgment of Solomon. Two women—harlots, the Bible calls them—came before King Solomon. They lived together and each had recently given birth to a baby son. One baby died. One woman claimed that the dead baby had been switched in the night with her live one. The other woman claimed the living baby was hers. So King Solomon said, "Bring me a sword." He ordered that the living baby be cut in two and each woman be given one half. At that, the true mother begged the king to spare the child and give him to the other woman; the false mother said, "Divide it." Solomon, of course, had the baby delivered to the first woman, saying, "She is its mother."[3]

Now in this case, as in many others, we have not one judgment but a series. The first—and crucial—one occurred in Solomon's mind, when he judged that to find the truth he must test each woman's love for the baby, and saw how to do it. Here he used his inmost self by drawing on pure memories (we don't know which ones) to produce a novel and useful action aimed at meaning (truth and justice). His later overt judgments—the pseudo one to use the sword and the real one to deliver the baby—were a playing out in the world of the first inward judgment.

The same inner-outer sequence holds true for most practical judgments, whenever the process requires more than rote or routine decisions. Whenever we must choose among unfamiliar or uncertain paths, and we summon the keenest of our inward powers to make the choice, we are activating our inmost self. This can be illustrated in a small way right now if the reader cares to play a little game. You are to find the shortest route to a lake-side camp. The camp is due north from the starting point. The road map, however, is split into segments. Therefore, you have to guess which route is shortest. Pick a route in the segment on this following page, using your best judgment about how to reach the due-north camp; then continue using the segments on succeeding pages. Don't turn the page until you have picked the route on the first map. Then use your best judgment on the second map, on the next page. It is best if you play the game seriously; otherwise it loses its point.

If you have now played this game, stop a moment and reflect on what went through your mind. One level of the game was deciding which route *looks* shortest. That is routine judgment. But then you probably began to wonder what sort of twist would the writer of this book put into such a game? How can I outguess him? And when you started pondering that—drawing on the practical wisdom allied to your pure memory store—then you were using your inmost self. The

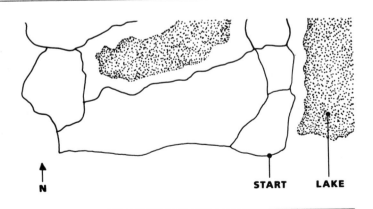

judgment you then made, based not simply on map reading but on your own psychologizing about the writer in an ambiguous situation, derived from the nonorganic part of you. The point of this game is not whether you guessed right or wrong but the *way* you did the guessing. Even in this little game, you can use the superconscious part of yourself.

Logical judgment, including the mathematical, amounts to an intuitive "seeing" of necessary relations. The ability to do this varies widely. All normal adults, though, possess extensive logical powers. You may not consider yourself gifted in logic, but you will undoubtedly "see" and accept the logical principle of the transitivity of identity, that is, within a single frame of reference, if A = B and B = C, then A = C. Some people come to "see" this principle by using an example.

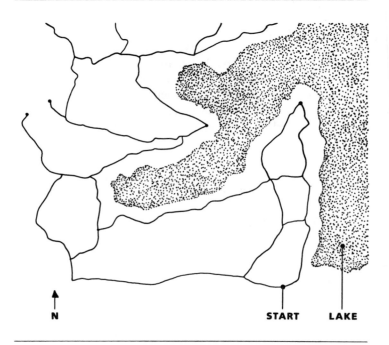

N   START   LAKE

Thus, one can suppose that Arthur weights 170 pounds and Bert weighs the same amount; and that Charles weighs the same as Bert. Then it follows that Charles, like Arthur, weighs 170 pounds. The transitivity of identity principle can also be proved rigorously by assuming its conclusion is false and showing that such an assumption leads to contradictions. Whatever way one comes to "see" the truth of a logical principle, that inward vision is a sign of one's inmost self in action.

Our logical powers develop naturally in childhood, as developmental psychologist Jean Piaget and others have discovered experimentally.[4] Thus Piaget found that, from the age of seven or eight, children begin to use what he calls the principle of conservation. In a famous experiment he showed that, when one pours water from glass A into a narrower glass B, a very young child (below seven) will say there is now more water—because it is higher in the narrow glass. In other words, as the child views it, the quantity of water has not been conserved. After seven or eight, on the contrary, the child will say: "It's the same water," or "It has only been poured," or "Nothing has been taken away or added," or "You can put the water in *B* back into *A* where it was before," or "The water is higher, but the glass is narrower, so it's the same amount." The child by then has mastered the principle of conservation of quantity, despite the changed appearances. This requires a new insight by the child's developing inmost self.

What is happening at this age, Piaget writes, is emergence in the child of an "epistemological subject" (a knowing I) who "becomes divorced from action proper so as to concern himself with the general coordination of action, i.e., with those permanent 'forms' of combination, overlapping, ordering, correspondence, etc., which relate actions to each other and thus constitute their necessary substructure." These logical "forms" cannot be explained mechanistically, Piaget affirms. So, too, arguably with some of the deep forms or structures used in language and the mental models used in science. They function not at the somatic or hedonic levels but noetically, where they serve as further contexts for logical judgments.

As for the "seeing" of mathematical judgments, Plato offers a famous example in the *Meno*. Socrates, in his inquiring way, brings an ignorant youth to see how to double the area of a square. Concluding that the boy had this knowledge without knowing that he had it, Socrates (Plato) reasons that it must come from recollection from an earlier existence, and

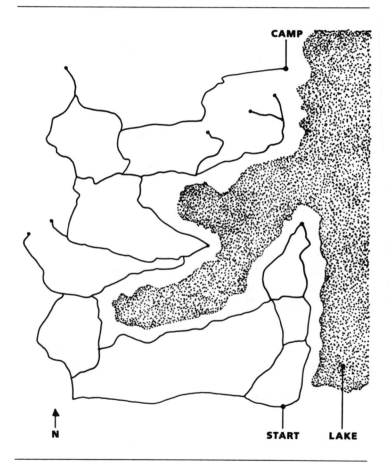

"if the truth about reality is always in our soul, the soul must be immortal."⁵

I would prefer a different conclusion, based on my own experience. This example of doubling the area of a square was new to me, too, when I read it, and I, like the boy, "saw" the answer as indubitable. That response had two stages. First, the drawings in the dialogue made the answer look right; this being a perceptual judgment. Second, I judged the answer *must* be right, based on the definition of a square and on a geometrical principle: that two triangles will be equal in area if all sides of one are identical in length to the sides of the other. Now it seems likely that I learned both this definition and this principle in high school geometry rather than in a previous existence. Thus what was called into play when I read the *Meno* may have been my long-ago personal pure memory, not my soul's unknown earlier existence.

Still unexplained, however, is the fact that one does "see" as self-evident the geometrical principle, just as one "sees" the transitivity of identity logical principle, and many others. Somehow the mind holds this power to recognize self-evident insights. This is not at all based on individual memories but is common to all intelligent human minds. We shall have more to say later about this power.

Moral judgments involve an oughtness. We can distinguish the kind of oughtness that grows out of manners or customs or prudence or authority from the moral ought. Thus a teenager may feel he ought to pop some "happy" drug because it is offered to him (good manners). Or he ought to try it because "everybody does" (contemporary customs). Or he ought not to pop it because he might be busted by the police (practical prudence). Or he ought not to do it because some father or mother figure forbade it (authority). Or he ought not to do it because it's wrong (moral judgment).

The moral quality in a situation is a summons or call to take an individual stand, a personal position. This in turn implies some freedom of choice. Without freedom, one has no morality. What moral judgment is available to an ant, a flea, a slug? They are imprisoned in reflex and instinct. For a human, whose limited freedom dwells in his noetic inmost self, moral judgment requires not simply an experience of oughtness but also some reflection in a perspective of right-and-wrong.

Why do we adjudge something morally wrong? Because it offends against our view of what we are or what we want to be (or, if some other agent is involved, it offends against our view of what that agent is or should be). This means that, even though certain moral rules may have been drilled into us as a child so that they are now largely subconscious schemata, our present moral judgment functions autonomously in the inmost self. It casts the proposed act up against an ideal model (which may be utilitarian, Christian, Marxist, or any other), seeking a harmony of act with model.

Admittedly, this is a narrow view of moral judgment, and the present discussion is absurdly truncated for so broad an area of human concern. However we are *only* seeking here to relate the activity of judging to the inmost self. If humans do engage in moral judgments of the kind described, these judgments often plausibly involve the inmost self, for they draw on pure memories to reach meaningful conclusions, using at times novel and useful ideas.

Aesthetic judgment is a certain way of responding to an object, a scene, an event, or an aggregation of them. It has been qualitatively defined as appreciating something for its own sake only. That is, one views the object from the standpoint of its internal relations and not from the standpoint of its practical, logical, moral, or other nonintrinsic value. This notion seems only partly correct. Each of the aesthetic object's internal relations also has links with events beyond the object. The more we know of these other links, fusing that remembered knowledge with the object's own internal *this*ness, the more complete our aesthetic response will be. Thus we get more aesthetic meaning from Renaissance religious paintings if we know the Gospel story than if we view these works solely as a harmony of colors, lines, and shadings.[6]

In any event, aesthetic response is a distinct though subtle capacity of the experiencing and inmost self. And every aesthetic experience is a novel one. Through training and temperament it can become quite intense. But is is also calm, unless it triggers some secondary response at the hedonic level. Aesthetic experience seems also to take one out of oneself. As the art historian Bernard Berenson describes it:

> Through my whole mature life . . . I have never enjoyed to the utmost a work of art of any kind, whether verbal, musical or visual, never enjoyed a landscape, without sinking my identity into that work of art, without becoming it, although . . . a minuscular observer is always there, watching, noting, appreciating, estimating, judging, always there in moments of utmost sensual and spiritual ecstasy and feeling with the rest, but still there.[7]

What actually happens in such an aesthetic experience? The aesthetic object is intentionally grasped in our experiencing self. We sink ourself into that. Our interactive area helps by suppressing all extraneous sense-data. The whole of our experiencing now embraces the art object. Our relating spreads within the perceived object and also summons memories from the inmost self. Aesthetic appreciation—a unique form of feeling—spreads from the inmost self to bathe our awareness. The veil between the inmost self and immediate experience seems almost to vanish, as in some creative acts. But still the subjective I, the supposed "minuscular observer," hovers separate. In this way, by "sinking oneself" into the art work, one absorbs that work into oneself, carrying it into the pure memory store, there to remain.

Cosmic judgment occurs when the larger context involved is the whole of reality. That is, we may judge that a certain experience is relating us directly to the primal nature or ground of the universe, or to *being* as such. The experience itself is often called mystical. Our interpretation of it is a cosmic judgment. On the other hand, we may reach cosmic judgments, not out of immediate experience but solely by way of thinking and willing. This happens when a study of philosophy or religion leads us to a certain belief about the universe or about being as such, in relation to specific objects (most notably oneself).

Mystical experiences have an immense range. Referring once again to our three criteria for inmost self involvement, by no means all mystical experiences draw on pure memories (except in the negative sense of "not this, not that"); but they are almost always interpreted as novel, useful, and intensely meaningful. Such experiences go from a simple feeling of union, a "cosmic consciousness," to the most fiery, vivid, and visionary trances. One of the simpler states is described by a scientist who wrote that as a young man he had a continuing "indefinite consciousness" of "an Absolute reality behind phenomena." When he had a life problem or felt depressed, he said, "I used to fall back for support upon this curious relation I felt myself to be in to this fundamental cosmical *It.*" This relation with the It "always strengthened me and seemed to give me endless vitality to feel its underlying and supporting presence." At the time he wrote, aged nearly fifty, his power of getting into connection with It had entirely left him and "I have to confess that a great help has gone out of my life."[8]

Berenson, the art historian, recounts a similar cosmic judgment based on an early experience of ecstatic harmony. In childhood, he reports, this ecstasy overtook him when he was happy out of doors. He recalls a morning in early summer, aged five or six, when "a silver haze shimmered and trembled over the lime trees. The air was laden with their fragrance. The temperature was like a caress." The boy climbed up a tree stump and "felt suddenly immersed in Itness. I did not call it by that name. I had no need for words. It and I were one." Often in adult years, Berenson reports, in moments when passion or ambition or self-righteousness seemed about to rule him, the feeling of that moment so long ago would present itself and "like a guardian angel remind me that IT was my goal and that IT was my only real happiness."[9]

T. S. Eliot in his poem "Burnt Norton" has tried to evoke the moment of mystical harmony and his judgment of its meaning:

> At the still point of the turning world. Neither flesh nor
> fleshless;

Neither from nor towards; at the still point, there the dance is,
But neither arrest nor movement. And do not call it fixity,
Where past and future are gathered. Neither movement from
   nor towards,
Neither ascent nor decline. Except for the point, the still point,
There would be no dance, and there is only the dance.[10]

A more inspirational type of mystical experience occurred
to the psychiatrist C. G. Jung at the age of sixty-nine, while
he hung close to death in a hospital after a heart attack. By
day, he writes, he felt weak and wretched. But at times in the
middle of the night, for a period of nearly three weeks, he
"floated in a state of purest bliss, 'thronged round with images of all creation.' " These visions "were the most tremen-
dous things I have ever experienced . . . We shy away from
the word 'eternal,' but I can describe the experience only as
the ecstasy of a non-temporal state in which present, past and
future are one." Seeking to define the experience, he calls it
"a state of feeling, but one which cannot be produced by imagination. How can I imagine that I exist simultaneously the
day before yesterday, today, and the day after tomorrow?
. . . One is interwoven into an indescribable whole and yet
observes it with complete objectivity."[11]

In our terms, Jung apparently was able to get into the fullness of his own be-ing, bringing into conscious awareness segments of his inmost self, a state that we may normally reach
only after death. Jung recovered from his illness, and thereafter, he writes, a fruitful period began for him. Some of his
principal works were written then. "The insight I had, or the
vision of the end of all things, gave me the courage to under-
take new formulations," he reports.

We shall have more to say about the meaning of mystical
experiences in Part Four. The point to be made here is that a
person's cosmic judgments, whether they stem from mystical
experience or philosophizing or a considered act of faith, cannot plausibly be reduced to brain functioning. This holds true
for the cosmic judgments of the skeptic and the religious
believer alike. Take for example the cosmic outlook expressed
by Bertrand Russell, as quoted in Chapter Two. There Russell
viewed humans as "but the outcome of accidental colloca-

tions of atoms," doomed to perish utterly as individuals, and in the end "all the labors of the ages, all the devotion, all the inspiration, all the noonday brightness of human genius, are destined to extinction in the vast death of the solar system . . . "

Here is a view derived from wide and thoughtful reading, organized by a powerful inmost self, presented with creative eloquence—none of which activities can plausibly be reduced to "accidental collocations of atoms." This statement, this cosmic attitude, emerged out of the nonorganic part of Russell's self. The same holds true for those who take a considered stand on the following words from Jesus of Nazareth: "Truly, truly, I say to you, he who hears my word and believes him who sent me, has eternal life; he does not come into judgment, but has passed from death to life." (John 5:24)

The person who takes a considered stand on these words, to accept them or reject them, must have employed his or her inmost self in making the judgment, just as Russell did in reaching his grim view. Such a stand would draw upon one's pure memories of accounts about the life and works of Jesus and discussions about the authority of Jesus; such a stand would hold a major place in one's search for meanings in life; and such a stand could produce novel and useful ideas for one's life. Those three criteria—a search for meanings that draws upon pure memories in helping to generate useful and novel ideas—are what we settled on in Chapter Fourteen as indicators of inmost self activity. Thus the person who takes a thoughtful stand on Jesus and eternal life, or on Russell and man as an accidental collocation of atoms, is employing his or her superconscious inmost self.

Likewise, as we saw, the inmost self engages in many practical, logical, moral, and aesthetic judgments. Likewise, it generates many acts of thinking, imagining, and willing. We can plausibly conclude, then, that *the superconscious inmost self is far more than a storehouse for memories. It is a highly active and creative part of us. If it persists beyond the death of the organism, then the part of us that survives will plausibly be active and creative.*

Before ending our exploration of the inmost self, let us note one overarching aspect of noetic experience that emerges from each of the past four chapters, namely the operation in people of a kind of inward light or light of the mind. One finds this in the *illumination* of the creative scientists, the imaginative *visions* of poets and painters, the youthful *insights* of men like Eccles and Mach that shaped their central inmost willing, and the ways our judgments *see* logical truth, artistic beauty, moral rightness, or cosmic reality. This inward light can be viewed as the power used by the subjective I in its thirst for meanings, as it relates and combines experiences, pure memories, and futural projections to generate new and useful ideas.

The light of the mind has been discussed by philosophers and religious thinkers at least since the time of Plato. The notion is embedded, too, in our language. Thus we say "I see" when we mean "I understand"; we speak of insight when we mean understanding. Let us be clear that "inward light" is a metaphor. We are comparing what happens within us, at the self's noetic level, with what happens outside us, in a world lit by physical light. In what ways are these happenings similar? For one thing, so far as our experience goes, both kinds of light function only part of the time. They function, in our experience, variably: sometimes bright, sometimes dim, sometimes leaving us in darkness. The greatest outward light, the sun, not only illumines but also warms, enabling organisms to grow. So too the inward light both illumines and enables the mind to grow.

Neither the outer light nor the inner light need be visible in itself. Rather, the light *makes visible*. Sunlight is the medium that reveals to us certain aspects of the world. Our eyes function *by means of* the light. We usually don't see the light itself. Indeed on a cloudy day it may be impossible to discover the source of light. Even so, the inward light—unseen itself—reveals to us images and relationships toward which we open our mind's eye.

A light of the mind seems to function in at least four major interrelated perspectives: truth, moral rightness, beauty, and love. Each of these provides us with its own kind of meaning. Using the inward light we see into events, feelings, ideas, or problems in a new way, revealing until-now-hidden meanings within one perspective or another. The insight into meaning may be positive or negative. One may see the newly grasped state of affairs as true or not-true, right or not-right, beautiful or not-beautiful, love or not-love. Also, each of us seems to have a different measure of light available. This varies with our differing endowments, experience, and skill in using the light. Thus the level of insight varies. Moreover, each illumination needs to be tested within its own perspective. Simply *having* a bright flash of insight offers no guarantee that it is valid.

Outward light comes from various sources: the sun, the moon, fire, electricity. Inward light comes from—what source? A hard question. Our subjective I *uses* this light, both in our experiencing self (in conscious insights) and in our inmost self (in superconscious insights, obtained during sleep or while we are occupied consciously with other matters). We use the inward light, then, but normally we cannot find its source. All we normally know of it is that at certain moments we are enlightened. It is as if we were permanently immersed in a certain milieu, a certain atmosphere, that makes itself known to us only through its effects.

19

The Experiencing Self–Perception

We turn now to a further aspect of mind in action, to examine the most striking thing about the experiencing self: its perceptions. In our waking hours we are almost always perceiving. How much do these perceptions stay with us? How fully are they preserved, rather than simply vanishing, once they depart from the conscious experiencing self? The survival hypothesis (in the naturalistic full-life version we have been developing since Chapter One) holds that many focal experiences—the ones we pay attention to—remain with us in pure memory, vivid and real behind the veil. If this is true, then our perceptions are not what they first seem. They are not direct experiencings of physical things. For we surely cannot take physical things into pure memory, holding them in our inmost self through our lifetime and beyond. So if we accept the full-life survival hypothesis, then we must expect to find something paradoxical about perceptions. And this we do discover. For example . . .

I am sitting on a bench with Irene. An autumn afternoon. I am conscious of the warm slanting sun, of Irene's words, of the scent she wears, of her leg where it touches mine, the mobile intelligence in her face. A yellow leaf falls in the sunlight. It rests now on her dark hair. I pluck the leaf from her head. I twirl it and present it to her. She smiles at me, a lovely smile, then goes on talking.

A series of perceptions. I have been seeing, hearing, touching, moving. More than that, I have had a series of small but meaningful experiences. Where did all this take place? If we harken to many of the important philosophers of the past three centuries, these perceptual experiences took place, not in an outer physical world but in the world of my consciousness.

But how could that possibly be? Weren't the two of us sitting on a real bench? Yes. Under a tree, out in the open, with the whole park around us? Yes. And Irene, isn't she a living real woman? Indeed yes. Then how could they all be *inside* me?

To explore this paradox of perception, we shall have to distinguish sharply between the physical world of atoms and molecules and the conscious world of direct experience. We have had an experiential description of what happened on the bench. Let us now try a physical description of what led to one particular event, my perception of the maple leaf alighting in Irene's hair:

Electromagnetic waves from the sun, of a certain frequency pattern, suddenly supplanted the waves of a different frequency pattern bouncing off part of the mass/energy location known as "Irene's hair." Some of these new-frequency waves penetrated my two eyes, struck the retinas, and activated their rods and cones in a leaf-shaped area. Neuronal activations, including several processing operations, led electrochemical impulses back through the right and left optic nerves, through jointure at the optic chiasm, traveling into and out of the central thalamus, and on to the visual areas of the right and left occipital cortex at the back of my brain.

All this occurred during a continuing complex series of other brain events. And here is the crucial point: I did not become aware of the yellow maple leaf on Irene's head, and recognize it, until *after* these data were transmitted from the physical location of "Irene's hair" through physical space to my eyes, through my retinas, my optic nerves, my thalamus, back to my occipital cortexes and then entered consciousness.

These facts seem to be well established by the evidence.[1] They imply that the physical event of the leaf landing in Irene's hair was separated in both time and space from the perceptual event of my becoming aware of the leaf landing in Irene's hair.

Thus if we take t_1 as the time of the physical event and t_2 as the time my retinas were activated and t_3 as the time the nerve impulses hit the optic chiasm and t_4 as the time the nerve impulses hit the thalamus and t_5 as the time they reached the right and left occipital cortexes, then the time when I perceived and recognized the leaf, after cortical processing, must have been at least t_6. So the leaf landing in Irene's hair (physically) and the leaf landing in Irene's hair (as I experienced it) were two quite different and separate events. They were evidently causally related; but they were no more the *same* thing than dropping a coin in a vending machine is the same thing as the soft drink that results.

As for space, the physical place of the leaf as it landed in Irene's hair, beside me on the bench, was clearly different from the physical place of the nerve impulses that finally reached my occipital cortexes, in the back of my head. The back of my head and the leaf on Irene's head were nearly a yard apart.

This perceptual paradox: that the "outside" world of my experience, the world of Irene, the bench, the park, the warm sunshine, the yellow leaf, the movement of my hand, her responding smile: all this, my experiential world, is *not* the physical world described by science as being truly there outside me, but rather unrolls "inside" me, a processed resultant of inward activity—this very paradox of perception has haunted modern thought ever since Descartes began his questioning three centuries ago.

What we are concerned with here, however, is not to "solve" the paradox. We simply need to find whether the most plausible view about what our perceptions are would permit our focal percepts to be carried into pure memory *as* they are. From this standpoint, we must ask: *Is it plausible that perceptual experiencings are reducible to brain action alone?* Here we need a further analysis of perceiving.

Neurological and psychological experiments suggest that perception is a constructive process and that it normally proceeds in two stages.[2] The first is very fast, crude, holistic, building on immediate sensations. This can rouse quick activity for alertness, fight or flight. This first perceptual stage seems to be largely if not wholly brain-generated. The second stage, by contrast, is deliberate, attentive, detailed, drawing on context, knowledge, and anticipation. This second stage yields our normal perceptual experiencing. The currency it deals in is meanings.

Whenever we grow aware of a complex meaning, some process higher than neuronal operations is plausibly at work. A meaning emerges when we fit a particular object or event into a larger context. The object gets identified, recognized, assigned a value, by us. If it were only a matter of fitting each object into a pigeonhole, brain activity might well suffice for the operation (as it may do in the simpler subconscious cases). But many meanings are complex and ambiguous; for them the prepared pigeonholes don't work. Moreover, our *awareness* of meaning requires a second, or reflective, level of organization. To know requires a knower as well as an object known. Things or events of the greatest rarity may occur in the world, but unless some aware knower—some subjective I—tunes them in, they can achieve no realized meanings. Thus a phonograph record of a Mozart symphony by itself is only a piece of hard vinyl. As processed by the brain, its sound waves are only a succession of neuronal agitations. As heard by an appreciative knower, it becomes music and takes on beauty and meaning.

Moreover, in experience we not only perceive objects and events; we also find nearly every moment bathed in one kind of feeling or another. And apart from percepts and feelings, our life world embraces at times recollections, thoughts, imaginings, dreams, fantasies, rehearsals, plans, judgments, decisions, strivings. Along with these different foreground events, our experience unrolls amidst a complex mental background.

As an example, let us return to the autumn afternoon when I sat with Irene on a bench. Earlier we followed my perception of a yellow leaf. It seemed to end up "inside" me. But what about Irene herself? Where was she, as I experienced her? She came into my experience in several ways. The view of her bright and mobile face, her dark hair, her smile, her body near me: all these came to me through light waves striking my retinas, then complex neuronal firings leading to the occipital cortex, as described. I also heard her tell me of her first love affair. The sound waves from her mouth went through the air to my ears, got analyzed somewhat in the chambers of my inner ears, proceeded through the thalamus to the right and left temporal cortex and perhaps beyond. I felt the touch of Irene's leg against mine, at times dully, at times with acute awareness. This came to me by neuronal chain firings up my leg, through the spinal cord, up through the thalamus to the top of my brain in the parietal cortex and perhaps beyond. In addition, various other brain systems were functioning, including my olfactory bulbs.

I had perceived Irene as a unity, varied and complex, but a single human being. However, these brain events—in widely separated parts of the brain—provided no unified percept. Far less did they furnish the other aspects of my experiencing of Irene. That experiencing included not only the sight of her body but my empathy with her as a person; not only the sound of her words but their meaning, and the pathos of that love affair, and the half-hidden inner question, why is she telling me this? The touch of her leg on mine led at times to a sweet tingling and to the thoughts, What is she feeling at this moment? Where is our friendship going? These thoughts and feelings interlaced with the Irene I saw and heard and with the background of the park around us.

Thus Irene as experienced was quite distinct from any set of widely separated activities in my brain, just as both sets of events were distinct and different from the female organism seated on a physical bench in physical space beside me. Irene-as-experienced emerged out of sensations generated and processed by widespread neuronal activity in my brain. But the brain action, though necessary, was not sufficient to create my experience of Irene. My experiencing of her ran along at a different level, fed not only by brain activity but by other sources, a level indescribable in terms of neuron groups and their activations. This new level, the level of meaningful experience, is most closely related to the contents and activities of the superconscious inmost self: to what we have explored at length as pure memory, creative thinking, imagining, willing, judging. We have already found a high plausibility for the view that pure memories are stored out of the brain, and at least a moderate plausibility for the view that significant activity in thinking, imagining, willing, and judging also occurs out of the brain. *We now find at least a moderate degree of plausibility that complex perceptions as well occur at an out-of-the-brain level.*

In effect, we have spent most of this inquiry to support the idea that mind and matter are distinct aspects of reality, that being-human is not reducible to brain and organism alone. In doing so, we have summoned empirical evidence for an insight held by many ordinary folk and by philosophers as well. This evidence indicates that *the meaningful core of each of us—our inmost self with its pure memories, its subjective I, and its varied activities in thinking, imagining, willing and judging, and much of our conscious experiencing as well—are not reducible to brain action, and therefore might persist beyond the death of the organism.* But how could this really happen? How *can* anything exist without a continuing physical basis? This ontological question, this ingrained sense of physical reality as fundamental, is the last and greatest hurdle facing any naturalistic belief in survival after death. We turn now to examine this question.

IV

Explaining the Evidence

20

The Reality of Time

After our long inquiry into empirical evidence bearing on the plausibility of human survival after death, we now ask whether survival as a natural fact can fit into a reasonable ontology or theory of reality. This is the course we charted in Chapter Three. But what is to count as reasonable here? A recent writer, Ian Barbour, in weighing ontological models, has suggested four criteria: simplicity, conformity to experience, coherence, and comprehensiveness.[1] These seem to me to be defensible criteria. As a guard against self-delusion, one might add that a reasonable ontology will draw upon at least one of the great streams of thought in philosophy.

We now seek a reasonable ontology into which survival after death can coherently and naturally fit. This must also answer the question posed at the end of the last chapter, namely: How *can* anything exist without a physical basis? The turn we now take, the path we explore, is by no means obscure or esoteric. It coheres with much recent philosophizing.

One major stream in twentieth-century thought might be called the philosophies of becoming. These philosophies include the phenomenological / existentialist movement, life philosophy, process thought, and pragmatism. Philosophers within this broad stream display wide variations. Nearly all of them, however, emphasize process more than stasis, existence more than essence, organism more than mechanism, history more than eternity, the changing more than the unchanging. Accordingly, most agree on the reality and centrality of time in human be-ing.

These philosophers generally consider that being reveals itself through becoming, through change-in-time, in contrast to the traditional stress on surpassing the changeable to reach eternal unchanging realities. Profound shifts in thought lie behind this altered approach. During the modern age, and especially from the nineteenth century onward, humans became aware as never before of how long our species has lived on earth, of the variety of cultures and the history of civilizations, of social and scientific progress, of biological evolution, of geological ages and changes, of the immensity and duration of the universe around us. We discovered not only progress but also, most basically, as philosophers Stephen Toulmin and June Goodfield put it, we discovered time, in its vast durational stretch.[2] This was public time; but its new importance validated the importance of becoming and of time as such.

This insight about the centrality of time may help us toward the ontology we seek. Perhaps time, rather than physical space, is the reality upon which or within which humans are founded. Perhaps time is not merely one dimension added to space, an imaginary straight line measuring succession, but marks out a realm of its own.

To get hold of this idea, however, requires a Copernican revolution in ordinary ways of thinking. Our measuring words are geared almost wholly to space. How shall we speak of time? A passage, a span, a long, a short, a distant time? All spatial words. The very clocks we use indicate time by a spatial shift in their pointers. But that is not the only problem. The time these philosophers are after is inward. This is the time of our life world, the time through which our direct experience flows. For this, Henri Bergson used the term *real duration* while Martin Heidegger, Jean-Paul Sartre, Maurice Merleau-Ponty, Edmund Husserl occasionally, and various others, use *temporality*. I shall employ *temporality* and, building on the philosophies of becoming, offer these answers to our ontological question:

The realm of temporality is the primary medium of all our experiencing and of our inmost mental life, as the realm of physical space is the primary medium of our organic life. *Medium* is used here to mean a universal environment; it is what we are always *in*. As one might say that water is the medium for fish or air the medium for birds, so temporality is the medium for human mental life.

Since temporality is a medium, it is not itself a measure. It thus differs from clock time, mathematical time, and the space-time of relativity physics, all of which reduce time to a one-dimensional measure. But *events* in temporality are, of course, subject to measurement.

We come upon a small pinch of temporality in the experiential present. This is the now of our experiencing self, normally amounting to some seconds of clock time, wherein we are aware not only of succession but also of a meaningful event being simply present. Thus someone may utter a sentence, "I'll give you a kiss if you close the door." On hearing this, you grasp the sentence's meaning as all there within the flow, even though by clock time the first words no longer exist at the moment when the last word has been heard and the meaning established. On a larger scale, take this present of your own experiencing and extend it back into the past and forward into the imagined future. Consider all of this as potentially available for knowing-all-together-right-now by the subjective I in the inmost self (as you knew-all-together the sentence offering the kiss). You then begin to grasp the quality of temporality.

Let us posit, with Heidegger, that in temporality each of us exists as stretched out between birth and death.[3] Moreover, for him, and for us, temporality is the ground or horizon that makes possible a meaningful human existence. As a metaphor (more Wittgensteinian than Heideggerian), temporality is the field on which one plays all the varied games that form one's life as a human being.[4] The length of this field is measured not in yards but in duration, in the temporal stretch of one's life; while the breadth of the field we can think of as the breadth (that is, the social or physical extensiveness) of events in one's life. Diagrammatically, we might envisage it like this:

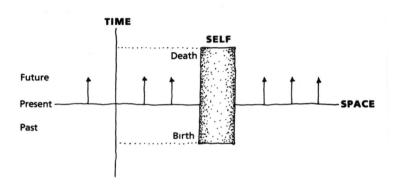

Figure 3. *The Self in Temporality*

This diagram derives from J. E. Orme, a psychologist who defends it with a wide variety of psychological and anthropological data.[5] The diagram represents two prime notions: (1) The self system has a real temporal stretch from birth to death. (2) Space moves forward through time; or, more accurately, the ultimate field for all physical interactions is temporal. We shall pursue this second point in a later chapter. Here let us explore the first point by examining the three modes of temporality—present, past and future—in relation to the existential self.

Present. The mode of "presencing" centers in the experiencing self; this has been discussed in Chapter Ten and elsewhere. Presencing occurs whenever anything makes itself present to one's awareness. This process has a temporal thickness to it, unlike the instantaneous mathematical present. Presencing must be conscious, for it is a coming-out-of-obscurity. At times the contents of presencing (intentional objects) seem thrust upon us, at other times we seek them out. The core content in presencing is usually clear and often sharply distinct. It is evident, undeniable. Surrounding this core, however, lies a foreconscious penumbra, as described in Chapter Ten. The penumbra relates in part to the core objects themselves, in part to the background against which they appear.

It was proposed in Chapter Ten that both the intentional objects in one's presencing and the penumbra around them emerge through an interactive area where the brain and mind come together. Like presencing, this subconscious interactive area presumably has some temporal thickness. The process of perception, for example, may involve a prehending in the present of the immediate physical past, as proposed by philosophers Henri Bergson and Alfred North Whitehead.

Past. We concluded in Part Two, to a high degree of plausibility, that each person retains somehow, outside the brain, a record of many of his or her past focal experiencings. Among the philosophers of becoming, Bergson has argued most strongly that these past records can be retained because *the past itself persists*. This is the simplest explanation for the facts about pure memory that we assembled in Part Two. It appears to be the most defensible one.

As our physical organism interacts with the physical environment and its own organs interplay among themselves—and as part of this activity feeds through the brain/mind interactive area and into our presencing awareness, generating perceptions, feelings, insights and imaginings—many of these key contents of our awareness do not vanish but remain as they were in temporality, while the physical processes move steadily forward through time, gnawing into the future. Thus are built up the past contents—the pure memories—of our superconscious inmost self. In a way this resembles those white contrails left behind in the upper air by a high-flying jet plane: as the plane zooms ahead, the contrails simply remain, until they slowly spread and dissolve. With us, however, many of the pure memories do not dissolve. They remain in the inmost self, part of the total system "who I am," part of the span covered by the subjective I or, to use an old word, part of my soul.

Why are we so little aware of the way our own past persists? Here, too, Bergson suggests a plausible answer. We are, he notes, practical creatures, geared to action in the world around us. Our life-needs depend primarily on the imminent future, not so much on the past. As Bergson put it: "The unperceived part of the material universe, big with promises and threats, has then for us a reality which the actually unperceived periods of our past existence cannot and should not possess."[6] Penfield, the neurologist cited earlier, also observed that the "experiential" recall of the past which he evoked in some patients would probably be highly disruptive to normal life. Thus an awareness of the past is largely blocked off by schemata in our brain/mind interactive area, to serve our futural orientation.

Some of those who affirm that the past persists would also affirm that it does so immutably. You cannot change the past, they say; it *is,* but as finished, dead, played out. This view of the past will not do for human beings. As we saw earlier, the pastward inmost self of humans is active, creative, a vigorously living, changing part of us. True, the past cannot be destroyed; but our interpretations and use of it shift and develop.

Moreover, a memory from ten or even twenty years ago may pop into awareness with no evidence at all that it has passed through intervening memories. This strongly suggests that the inmost self has a systemic organization in temporality that goes far beyond any limited serial ordering of memories. At the same time, it seems reasonable to hold to the usual postulate in natural science, that no gaps occur between cause and effect. If this is so, and if my personal past does stretch out behind me, persisting back through the years of my life, and if I do manage to recall now certain events from long ago, then some kind of field must operate over this whole backward stretch of my inmost self: that is, my pastward self is not just a series of pure memories but a highly organized system with its own fields, each field having its net of communication rules. Indeed, some such view seems implied by the many complex usages of pure memory we reviewed in Part Three.[7]

In the light of all this, we should abandon the notion of one's persisting personal past as frozen or dead.

Future. We all deal with the future, in projections I shall call "futuring." Does this mean that one's future already exists in temporality? Let us consider some examples.

I am going to a party at a new friend's house, and I get from him directions on how to drive there. I make a mental map of the street names, distances, and turns. When I drive, I follow this mental map, even though it is not now in my awareness. I may look at the passing scenery, watch the traffic, chat with my companion, but all the while I am guided by the out-of-awareness map, for at the crucial points I switch attention and ask myself: "Do I turn here?" It is as if this map were projected out ahead of my presencing-field (that is, the field of my present experiencing), sketched into my imminent future.

However, all such small plans involve making preparations in a present that now is past and carrying them out in a future that becomes present. Thus one might claim that I simply recall the plan out of my memory; but this does not seem to be so when I am doing it. Rather, the plan is projected out ahead of my consciousness, that is, I am futuring it. This is shown by the fact that the plan sequentially dissolves as the advancing physical events overtake it.

Indeed, in ongoing action, we often test what is currently happening against a future projection. Thus, in playing a bridge hand, my opponent on the left may suddenly trump a trick, revealing a short suit. I then cast this new information against my projected strategy and see whether I need to change strategy. So it goes, too, with a host of other projections, in ongoing activity. Broadly speaking, we can describe what happens as follows: The experiencing self perceives a new situation; this is cast up against a futural project in the inmost self; the subjective I centered in the pastward inmost self then "reads" the new data against the futural project and interprets the situation accordingly.

At a deeper level, the final anticipation in this life, as Heidegger says, is our own death, the making-a-whole of

Dasein (human existence). Whenever we consider our death as a real prospect (a hard thing for most of us to do), we are futuring. That is, we are peering into our own future, as we also do when we anticipate in detail a future trip to Europe, the giving of a lecture, the birth of our coming child. In each case we stretch our own temporality ahead of us to the significant future date. We think of preparations to make. Various anticipatory feelings arise in us.

Moreover, each of us has a few major projects that guide and organize our life. These projects are goals to achieve; they are examples of the central willing discussed in Chapter Seventeen. These are things to do; but we also have a project to *be*. That is, we hold a particular style of person as our ego ideal, the project for our selfhood. We may have modeled this long ago on an idealized parent, teacher, or other admired adult. Often the model, and even the nature, of the ego ideal stays obscure to us. Yet it guides our style in facing the future.

Creative imagining offers further examples of futuring, some of which we came upon in Chapter Sixteen. A writer may imagine in detail the plot, characters, settings, tone, and impact of a story or novel he hopes to create. A painter may envisage the subject and balance of forms and colors in his next painting. A composer may find melodic fragments gathered into a full panorama in his mind. All these cases involve creative works still to be made. These imaginings become, in effect, plans for future action; thus they are futural, they direct the artist's future life insofar as he or she takes them seriously and embarks upon them.

In this light, we see that small plans, anticipations, major projects, and acts of imagining all have, as their referents, not-yet-actualized possibilities. These referents (that is, the goals themselves) may in due time become part of one's presencing, then move into pastward memories. Now, however, they are future possibles.

What shall we say generally about the existence of one's futural projects? Let us define *to exist* as to participate in the activity of be-ing in temporality (I shall justify this definition later, in Chapter Twenty-Three). Unlike the presencing mode, which exists, and the pastward mode, which also exists, these futural projects seem to have only a limited hold on existence. Our futurings are real as possibilities (except for those that are impossible, such as imagining that I shall meet a hippogriff around the next corner); but they exist only as signs, as not-yet-fulfilled claims that their referents will become actual.

Granted that fact, however, the more interesting discovery about futuring may be this: It seems that we have a futural field, open and available to receive our projections and imaginative conceivings, and the simplest most plausible way to integrate this futural field into the self is to regard it as part of the superconscious inmost self.[8] If our projections were kept in conscious awareness, we should count them as part of the experiencing self. If they were habitual schemata, we might count them as part of the subconscious interactive area. But these projections are, for the most part, neither conscious nor habitual. Most belong, then, in the inmost self. Thus the inmost self system extends not only back through our pastward life but also forward into the open futural field. Temporally speaking, the inmost self surrounds the experiencing self and its penumbra and the brain/mind interactive area. This confirms Heidegger's insight that human existence stretches along in temporality all the way from birth to death. It fits with the diagram presented a few pages back. It fits into an early insight by Bergson, who affirmed in 1912 that—because of this temporal stretch—"the mind overflows the brain on all sides" and "cerebral activity responds only to a very small part of mental activity."

What we have found is that human brain systems are immensely complex in their physical organization in space; but the brain as an *existent* has a very short temporal duration (my brain of half an hour ago exists no longer).[9] By contrast the mental side of the self is not only systemically complex, but the inmost self has a long durational existence running pastward back to one's earliest memories. As for futural spread, the inmost self projects possibilities, but the brain, though it generates possibilities, gives no evidence of projecting them. That is, the brain seems to operate with past-formed programs of skills, reflexes, and instincts, rather than by creating future projects as does the mind. Thus Bergson was right in affirming that the mind "overflows" the brain temporally on all sides. And he drew an obvious conclusion:

> . . . . if there were equivalence between the cerebral and the mental, consciousness might be bound up with the destiny of the brain and death might be the end of all . . . . But if, as I have tried to show, the mental life overflows the cerebral life, if the brain does but translate into movements a small part of what takes place in consciousness, then survival becomes so probable that the onus of proof falls on him who denies it rather than on him who affirms it; for the only reason we can have for believing in the extinction of consciousness at death is that we see the body become disorganized, that this is a fact of experience, and that reason loses its force if the independence of almost the whole of consciousness with regard to the body has been shown to be also a fact of experience.[10]

Bergson here uses *consciousness* to include what we have called the superconscious, and *body* to denote the organism. Apart from this small difference, however, he had already by 1912—drawing on a much smaller scientific data base than we now possess—reached very similar conclusions to those of the present inquiry. If one accepts those conclusions, all of them based on careful weighing of evidence, then Bergson's deduction also seems reasonable: that survival becomes so probable (or plausible) that the onus of proof falls on the doubter, not on the believer.

But even granted all this, aren't we dealing here with a far too narrow ontology? How does the whole great world, both physical and social, fit with this temporalized view of the nature of human existence? That question we still must consider. Before tackling it, however, we turn to a more pressing and intimate topic: From the point of view now reached, from what we have so far learned about the self and about human be-ing in temporality, what kind of survival might we plausibly anticipate after death?

21

What Kind of Survival?

Peace, peace! he is not dead, he doth not sleep—
He hath awakened from the dream of life—
'Tis we who, lost in stormy visions, keep
With phantoms an unprofitable strife . . . .

He has outsoared the shadow of our night;
Envy and calumny, and hate and pain,
And that unrest which men miscall delight,
Can touch him not, and torture not again.
                              Shelley, *Adonais*

We now are able to claim with at least moderate plausibility
that each person's inmost self lives on indefinitely in temporality. This is a minimal claim as to survival after death. It is a
claim advanced and sustained solely on naturalistic grounds.
There may be much more to survival than we here propose.
Several great religions assert that there *is* much more. The
reader, drawing on theology, revelation, and faith, can add as
he or she sees fit to what is about to be set forth. Nonetheless,
what we are here able to deduce about the reality and the
nature of survival seems of major human significance.

We have come here by a long route. All of our journey was needed to make the claim of survival naturalistically plausible. We have found that a person's pure memories—that is, one's memories of individual events and insights—seem to have no storage place in the brain. We found, too, that people retain pure memories even from childhood and even when they cannot normally bring them into awareness. We noted that the inmost self—what carries one's personal identity—is intimately tied to one's pure memories.

Examining perception, we discovered that percepts are not the physical things they purport to be, nor are they reducible to brain neurons. As with memories, one's percepts—indeed all of our experiences—come to one in a personal time that we have called temporality. We found it plausible to distinguish three segments of the whole self—organic, experiencing, and inmost—with an interactive area linking them, and with the subjective I dwelling in the superconscious inmost self.

Exploring the inmost self, we uncovered many examples of its creative activity—in thinking, imagining, willing, and judging. We discovered, too, that the subjective I in the inmost self shows a thirst for meaning. It uses not only the past but the future of temporality for its projects. And it has a capacity for insight or illumination that has been called an inward light.

All these aspects of being human beckon us to this conclusion: *One's inmost self need not go down to death with one's organism.* The inner person grew with one's organism, it interacts with organism, but it is not reducible to organism. It dwells not in physical space, like the organic self, but in the realm of temporality.

Our inquiry gives strong hints, also, about the kind of existence we may reasonably expect after death. When one dies, on this hypothesis, the long and fruitful interaction between the brain / organism / environment and one's inmost self terminates. One's brain-to-mind interactive area is wrenched apart. All experiencing retreats to the inmost self. One's participation in the realm of physical space and energy is over. All new perceptions of the world are over. The emotions, feelings, desires that are welled up from the organism to guide, delight, and sometimes torture one—all these are gone, as are the pains and anguish. The life force that roused us each morning and sent us forth into the world is gone, gone. All these are mortal. All these are lost in dying.

What we lose is the *future* of these organic powers. We do not lose their past. What we have experienced as a child, as a yearning adolescent, as a young person making friends, seeking love, embarking on work—these focal experiences of our past, down through the years to the day of our death—all these remain with us in life after death. These are the pure memories of the inmost self. We have them today; we shall carry them with us beyond the grave. For these do not dwell in the brain but in our stretch of temporality. Let us recall what we found in Part Two. Think of the people who, under hypnosis, summoned back some long-forgotten childhood event. Think of those others who have suffered massive electroshock, epileptic *grand mal* seizures, surgical lobotomies, surgical removal of brain "memory areas"—and still their memories returned. Clearly our pure memories do not perish with our brain, because they are not *in* the brain. We take them with us in temporality.

It seems likely that these pure memories subsist with far more vividness and liveliness "behind the veil" (as Penfield discovered with his patients) than they do in the faint images most of us now call memory. For us the living, pulled inexorably toward action and the world, the interactive area does normally interpose a veil against too-vivid memories. But in postmortem life the interactive area is gone, no veil exists, we enter a realm (as Fechner suggested) of being always awake; on whatever memory our subjective I then alights, it knows all of what the moment holds.

Some people experience this state occasionally while alive. One who did so was the novelist Marcel Proust. In his seven-volume master-work, *Remembrance of Things Past,* Proust reports certain trivial perceptions—the taste of a madeleine cake soaked in tea, stumbling on a flagstone, the sound of a spoon striking a plate, the feel of a starched napkin—which evoked a former situation or event with fully vivid reality, "as if they were occurring simultaneously in the present moment and in some distant past." Marcel, in the novel, experienced these evocations with inexplicable joy. Only toward the end did he conclude that the joy came from discovering, through this power of memory, that within him dwelt an inner person who would not die.[1]

But surely a novel is no real evidence? In Proust's case, however, these evocative events were based on real experiences, which he described in a 1909 preface to another book. He proposed that such pure memories are reality itself, "a fragment of pure life preserved in its purity, which we can only know when it is so preserved, because, in the moment when we live it, it is not present to our memory, but surrounded by sensations which suppress it."[2] Thus, for Proust, pure memory forms a reality even more vivid and meaningful than the original experience.

There are some further reasons, too, why our postmortem awareness may be broader and more meaningful than what we are accustomed to. Normally in daily life our consciousness is not only focussed and narrowed by outside demands; it is also moved by thirst for life and pleasure. But the somatic and hedonic thrusts as they intensify in us tend to diminish our conscious awareness. Intense physical action of any kind pulls us into itself, away from our subjectivity. At the climax of the sexual act, for example, one is scarcely aware of oneself at all; one is plunged into pure feeling. So too with intensities of pain: these may literally drive one unconscious. But the realm of the inmost self (and postmortem self) does not move internally by thirst for life or pleasure. It moves internally only by thirst for meaning. And this thirst at its peak evokes not unawareness but ever broader and deeper awareness: as with Kekulé and his twisting snakes, Crick and Watson with their double helix, Cardan and his "absurd" imaginaries, Mozart composing a symphony, Mach and his world-insight on a summer's day, Damien and his life-choice, Blake seeing "through" his eye, Jung grasping the temporality stretch of his visions.

These are the reasons for saying that the postmortem I (which is simply the subjective I continued) will be aware more broadly and meaningfully than what we are used to here and now: because the thirst for meaning will then be controlling, rather than the demands of environment or of thirst for life or pleasure.

One may ask, how can we be aware at all after death, in light of the statement, as far back as Chapter Ten, that conscious awareness occurs only in the experiencing self and that the inmost self is "superconscious"? The answer to this objection runs as follows: Awareness depends on an interaction of the subjective I with a mental object or objects. This awareness is conscious when the object(s) appear in the experiencing self. It is superconscious when the object(s) dwell in the inmost self. Superconscious awareness can become more or less conscious, in ordinary life, when its object flows through the interactive area and into the experiencing self. The subjective I, though, can never be consciously grasped: for that, it would have to be an object, and it is always a subject, always the "who" that experiences, never the "what" that is experienced, as pointed out in Chapter Ten.[3] It seems plausible that the subjective I is formed by interaction of the contents of the experiencing and inmost self with something more basic, impelled especially by thirst for meaning.[4] This interaction steadily builds a subjective I that, for each one of us, spreads throughout our inmost self. As it develops, the subjective I in turn becomes active and exploratory, increasing its own awareness. After death, if this view is correct, the subjective I, the contents of the inmost self, and the thirst for meaning continue to interact, producing ever greater superconscious awareness.

Already, in the chapters on intellect, imagination, will, and judgment, we have glimpsed some kinds of activity that the postmortem I may engage in. After death the intellective insights attained in life will still remain in one's inmost self, as well as one's vast life imagery. Now, postmortem, one may actively interrelate these, just as living thinkers do. Thus one can derive new and changed insights about reality and meaning.

Imaginatively, too, one may reassemble and rearrange parts of this great conglomeration of pure memories and ideas. As in a daydream or a work of art, we can make of these what we will, whatever seems to us meaningful. But we cannot destroy what has been. And the will? The postmortem will, of all the powers of the inmost self, seems to lose the most by loss of the organism and the world. It can no longer impel action in the world. It serves now only the thirst for meaning, and this implies that it serves primarily the judgment.

In life, when facing a decision, how often we think, "But I don't know the boss's view, so how can I decide?" or "I'll do this, nobody will find out," or "I wonder if Jane won't hate me for it," or "Damn the torpedoes, full speed ahead!" For the postmortem I, not only life's acts and omissions but also many of their results are present for judging. They stare at us, those life-decisions, bare now and unconcealed, bereft of wishful excuses, demanding to be judged so their final meaning may emerge. And in these judgments—using practical, logical, moral, aesthetic, and cosmic criteria—our postmortem I builds slowly toward its ultimate realization. It comes to see (not perfectly, but as well as it finally can) the meaning of what *we* are in all our relationships. We then stand revealed, to our own post-mortem I, based on the meanings of all we did and failed to do in our now-preserved once-lived past. And so, though our imagination and intellect may continue indefinitely to find new creative materials, it seems our postmortem judgment of *ourself* must reach a final settled conclusion: our life on earth was what it was, this is what we hoped for, these were the obstacles, this is what we did with it, here is what it meant. This final unblinking judgment of *ourself* as we lived, by our own subjective I, goes with us in temporality onward and onward. We cannot escape it. It *is* ourself as we and the world made us.

Does this seem a lonely prospect? It should not. For we shall be dwelling not only with our postmortem I but also with our focal memories and insights about those whom we have known. We shall be aware of how they looked, what we and they did, the interchange of feelings and thoughts: and this not at one time only but throughout our whole relation-

ship. Thus the closer we have been to someone, the more he
or she survives with us. Indeed, someone we know well may
"come alive" more fully to our postmortem I (as Proust sur-
mised) than he or she does today—not in the physical sense,
of course, but as a *person* of vivid appearances and meanings
stretched out in temporality.

To what degree will another person—say one's wife or husband—appear to one bodily after one's death? Quite fully
—at least as completely as one might hallucinate the other
person here and now. Our pure memory of the other's body
—as we saw it, touched it, heard the voice, caressed and
smelled the hair, felt the warmth of a kiss—all this, in the
many guises we have experienced, can return to us whenever
we summon it. And the same holds true for our own body.
Our organism exists no more; our body image remains. Actually not one body image but a myriad; many of the ways we
are focally aware of our body during life, all the pure
memories that we have linked relationally to the notion "my
body," all these are available to our superconscious awareness. There is no reason to describe postmortem existence as
"disembodied." Nonorganic, to be sure; but our body-as-
perceived, at all ages, remains with us, and we may inhabit it
as we will. So, too, with the places, the possessions, and the
animals we have intimately known.

To what degree will we have feelings after death? Here, if
the full-life hypothesis is correct, we must distinguish between
memory of feelings (which will survive with us) and new feelings. There is substantial evidence, as we noted in Chapter
Eleven, that feelings originate from events in the organism
and the interactive area. If this is so, no new feelings can be
generated naturally after death. Nor can remembered feelings, then, regenerate new emotion out of the organism, as
now they often do. This means that postmortem one can expect to feel no sexual or other bodily pleasures; but neither
will one experience pain, hate, fear or other forms of bodily
distress.

One kind of feeling, though, is an exception and seems likely not only to persist but to extend itself, after death. This is a
gentle feeling, so gentle that some would claim it does not

exist. Others describe it as joy or bliss. We name it the "unity feeling." We referred to it in the section on cosmic judgment, in Chapter Eighteen. For a scientist and for Berenson, an art historian, this feeling accompanied an experience of being in touch with a cosmic It. The feeling, thus, seems to go along with transcendence. Some call it a cosmic consciousness. Nature writers have described it, among them Wordsworth:

> And I have felt
> A presence that disturbs me with the joy
> Of elevated thoughts; a sense sublime
> Of something far more deeply interfused,
> Whose dwelling is the light of setting suns,
> And the round ocean and the living air,
> And the blue sky, and in the mind of man;
> A motion and a spirit, that impels
> All thinking things, all objects of all thought
> And rolls through all things.[5]

Or Thoreau:

> In youth . . . this earth was the most glorious musical instrument, and I was audience to its strains. To have such sweet impressions made on us, such ecstasies begotten of the breezes! I can remember how I was astonished. I said to myself—I said to others—There comes into my mind such an indescribable, infinite, all-absorbing, divine, heavenly pleasure, a sense of elevation and expansion, and I have had nought to do with it. I perceive I am dealt with by superior powers . . . . With all your science can you tell how it is, and whence it is, that light comes into the soul?[6]

Richard Jefferies, an English writer, tells of a unity experience, while he lay on the grass as a young man:

> Having drunk deeply of the heaven above and felt the most glorious beauty of the day, and remembering the old, old sea, which (as it seemed to me) was but just yonder at the edge, I now became lost and absorbed into the being or existence of the universe. I felt down deep into the earth under, and high above into the sky, and farther still to the sun and stars. Still farther beyond the stars into the hollow of space, and losing my separateness of being came to seem like a part of the whole.[7]

The unity feeling may be evoked not only by nature but also by aesthetic experiences or by problem-solving or by awakening to love.[8] Various mystics have experienced it as a kind of sweet emptiness or nothingness. Among medieval mystics, Tauler described this as "a fathomless sinking into a fathomless nothingness." Eckhart spoke of entering a state of "pure nothingness," in which one sinks "from negation to negation in the One." Ruysbroek found a "limitless abyss" of the Godhead, "so naked of all image," and "there we feel that our spirits are stripped of all things and bathed beyond all thought of rising in the pure and infinite ocean of love."[9]

Since the unity feeling can arise with or without organic tensions, one may plausibly argue that it originates not from the brain or the interactive area but from the same basic source as our thirst for meaning. In that case the unity feeling is directly available to the inmost self, both before and after death.

And yet . . . I haven't experienced any of this postmortem realm. How can I talk so confidently about it? Well, I am simply trying to develop the most inclusively reasonable view of things, based on facts uncovered by science and human experience. That is all we have been about in this inquiry. It seems most reasonable to believe that if the inmost self does not dwell in the brain, if its nature differs from entities defined by physical space and mass/energy (as the evidence seems to show), then it should be able to continue in temporality after severance of its ties with the brain, with space, and with mass/energy. In effect, I am simply proposing that the principle behind Newton's first law of motion applies analogously to the realm of temporality as well as to the realm of physical space. Newton's law declares: Everybody continues in its state of rest or of uniform motion in a straight line if no force acts upon it. (In relativity physics, the principle of conservation of momentum is not only preserved but taken as a fundamental assumption).[10] Applying this principle to the realm of temporality: The "body" at issue here is our inmost self, its "motion" derives from thirst for meaning expressed by the subjective I, and when the "force" of demands from the organism has disappeared, then the movement toward meaning freely continues. That is the fundamental principle I have followed.

In addition, there is a whole class of positive evidence that claims contact with other persons, living and dead, by extrasensory means. As yet we haven't touched on this topic of extrasensory perception (ESP). I have wanted to see how far we could move into the inmost self and the postmortem self by means of ordinary kinds of empirical evidence. Now, though, we should consider the nonordinary empirical evidence.

22

Extrasensory Experience

Over the past century many accounts of alleged extrasensory experience have been published. Some of these accounts are anecdotal; others describe experiments, either careful or cursory. Here we shall consider, very briefly, only four types of nonordinary experience that relate most closely to the survival hypothesis.

The four areas to be explored are telepathy between the living, communications with the dead, persons returning from death, and cases of apparent reincarnation. Telepathy between the living, or mind reading, is relevant here because if this process can occur, and if the inmost self of each of us does survive death, then it seems quite possible that telepathy also occurs among postmortem selves. Moreover, telepathy should work more easily post-mortem, after death dissolves the brain-mind interactive area and its restrictive schemata.

This makes it plausible—if telepathy does exist—that our postmortem selves communicate with other such selves. Such contact should flow most fully with those persons we have been close to during our lives, for it is always simpler to communicate with someone based on shared experiences, especially after any emotional roadblocks (in the interactive area schemata) have been dissolved. Thus, if telepathy does exist, we can plausibly suppose that postmortem awareness is not only personal but social. Those dear to us in life can return to us after death not only through vivid memory, as proposed in the last chapter, but also in new direct communications. Indeed, of the four areas of extrasensory experience we are examining, telepathy holds by far the greatest importance for our full-life hypothesis, because of what it suggests about a socialized survival after death.

How strong is the evidence for telepathy among the living? Quite strong, in my opinion. However, only a few people among educated, sophisticated adults have been shown to enjoy great telepathic abilities. The practical, factual, materialistic thrust of modern education and modern life probably inhibits most sophisticated people's extrasensory powers, here and now. Based on sparse evidence, telepathic sensitivity may be stronger among children and nonsophisticated adults. But we do know of some remarkable clearcut cases of telepathy. Here are three such examples:

In 1928 and 1929 the novelist Upton Sinclair and his wife experimented at length with Mrs. Sinclair's psychic powers.[1] In the chief set of experiments, Sinclair (or occasionally his secretary) would draw a picture of an object, out of sight of his wife. Several of these drawings would be separately wrapped in opaque green paper. When she was ready, Mrs. Sinclair would take the wrapped drawings, put them on a table by her couch, lie down, pick up one wrapped drawing, and place it on her solar plexus, covered by her hand. She would then concentrate, obtain an image, draw it on a pad, sometimes add descriptive words, then repeat the process for other drawings on the table. Sinclair often watched his wife during this process. He reports that "she left no loophole for self-deception." He notes, too, that his drawings included a great variety of imagined objects.

When Mrs. Sinclair had finished, they unwrapped the original drawings and compared hers with these. Figure 4 reproduces several of these pairs, taken from Sinclair's book on the subject. In each case Sinclair's drawing is on the left or above; Mrs. Sinclair's attempted copy is on the right or below. Altogether, out of 290 drawing pairs, Sinclair credits his wife with success in 65 cases, partial success in 155 and failure in 70. Another professional investigator later confirmed this classification.

Such an achievement seems impossible by chance. It must show either strong extrasensory powers or fraud. Albert Einstein, in a preface to the first edition of Sinclair's book, suggests that "it is out of the question in the case of so conscientious an observer and writer as Upton Sinclair that he is carrying on a conscious deception of the reading world." As for unconscious deception—for example, involuntary whispering by Sinclair of the name of what he had drawn—this seems ruled out by the fact that many of Mrs. Sinclair's drawings, though they *looked* like his, were meant by her to portray a wholly different object from the one he had actually drawn.

Sinclair's book leaves unanswered whether his wife practiced clairvoyance (directly imaging a physical thing) or telepathy (imaging her husband's percepts or pure memories). Telepathy is the simpler explanation and seems preferable. Telepathy is suggested, too, by Sinclair's report that "my wife's drawings sometimes contain things which are not in mine, but which were in my mind while I was making them, or while she was 'concentrating.' " Also at times Mrs. Sinclair reproduced one of Sinclair's drawings right after he made it, in a distant room —or she imaged a drawing just made by her brother-in-law in his own home forty miles away.

A wholly different kind of experiment was carried out in the mid-1950s by an English mathematician, S. G. Soal, and his collaborator, H. T. Bowden.[2] During summer holidays in a Welsh village, Soal got acquainted with two boys, first cousins named Ieuan and Glyn. Soal had long been involved with ESP research and he discovered that Ieuan and Glyn, both aged thirteen, were gifted telepathically. He and Bowden tested them with packs of twenty-five standard cards. The cards pictured five different colored animals, with each animal repeated five times in the pack. After shuffling, Ieuan would be shown a card; Glyn, separated and screened from him, would guess what animal the card pictured. By jollying

Figure 4. Reprinted from Upton Sinclair, *Mental Radio*
(Springfield, IL: Charles C. Thomas, 1930 and 1962),
by permission of David Sinclair, copyright holder.

the boys along, and paying them prize money for high scores, Soal and Bowden persuaded them to continue this "guessing game" for two years. The experimenters took every precaution against cheating, including use of independent observers. At first the trials occurred indoors. Then they were shifted outside near the village, with the two boys moved apart sixty feet and then 166 feet. Trials were also organized in London, on the playing field of St. Paul's School.

Altogether the boys made 15,348 trials of the cards. The expected mean score of correct calls, by chance, would be one fifth, or 3,070. The actual number of correct calls by Glyn was 5,461 or 2,391 more than expected by chance. This gives a critical ratio of 47, Soal reports. That is, the likelihood of these results occurring by chance is almost infinitesimal. Interestingly, the boys scored even higher in the outdoor trials, where cheating was least possible, than they did in the indoor ones. Early on, the boys did try cheating once; this was promptly caught and squelched by Soal and Bowden, who cut off communications for several months thereafter. It seems likely, as Soal affirms, that no further cheating took place. These findings are the strongest statistical evidence for telepathy that I am aware of. Soal suggests, however, that "there are many such pairs as Glyn and Ieuan," so far undiscovered.

A third kind of example comes from the Dream Laboratory at Maimonides Medical Center in Brooklyn, New York. Montague Ullman, a psychiatrist, and Stanley Krippner, a psychologist, conducted a series of experiments there on dream telepathy.[3] One of the subjects was Malcolm Bessent, a young English psychic, who scored remarkably in a mass telepathy dream experiment set up by the Maimonides group. The mass telepathy was staged by a rock band, "The Grateful Dead," during six concerts they gave in early 1971 at a theater in Port Chester, New York. Each evening during the concert the audience—some 2000 rock fans—was advised on a slide: "Try using your ESP to 'send' this picture to Malcolm Bessent . . . now at the Maimonides Dream Laboratory in Brooklyn." A slide picture, chosen randomly on the spot from fourteen pictures, was then projected to the audience for fifteen minutes, while The Grateful Dead continued to play.

Bessent, meanwhile, slept peacefully in the Brooklyn laboratory forty-five miles away. He was installed in a sound-isolated room, with electrodes attached to his head. These alerted the experimenter in a nearby room whenever Bessent began rapid eye movement (REM) sleep, which usually indicates dreaming. At the end of the REM sleep period following each rock concert projection, the experimenter would awaken Bessent. The young Englishman would then tape-record an account of his dream and go back to sleep.

Bessent in this experiment scored four "direct hits" out of six nights. On the second night, for example, the picture projected to the rock audience was "The Seven Spinal Chakras" by M. K. Scralian. This shows a man in the yogic lotus position, apparently seated in mid-air. The seven chakras (purported energy centers keyed to the spinal column) are vividly colored. Brilliant yellow mosaics of energy radiate from a sunlike sphere atop the man's head, dominating the picture. While this image was beamed to the rock audience, Bessent dreamed:

> I was very interested in . . . using natural energy . . . I was talking to this guy who said he'd invented a way of using solar energy and he showed me this box . . . to catch the light of the sun which was all we needed to generate and store the energy . . . I was discussing with this other guy a number of other areas of communication and we were exchanging ideas on the whole thing . . . He was suspended in mid-air or something . . . I was thinking about rocket ships . . . I'm remembering a dream I had . . . about an energy box and . . . a spinal column.

From these and other accounts we can conclude with high plausibility that telepathic communication is a fact among some persons here and now. As Ullman and Krippner point out, it seems to flow most easily between those who have shared in love and sympathy while alive.

What shall we make of alleged communications by living persons with the dead? Many mediums or psychics have claimed to utter messages from the dead. Ever since the founding of the Society for Psychical Research in London in 1882, serious efforts have been made to test these assertions.

Some mediums were exposed as frauds. A few others persuaded the most diligent investigators, including William James, that they had attained some kind of contact with post-mortem selves. The most detailed and intricate communications came from the purported spirit of Frederic W. H. Myers, a prominent British psychical researcher, who died in 1901. This testimony has been ably summarized by Gardner Murphy, a leading American psychologist and a notably hard-headed man.[4] Murphy concluded:

> Struggle though I may as a psychologist, for forty-five years, to try to find a "naturalistic" and "normal" way of handling this [Myers] material, I cannot do this even when using all the information we have about human chicanery and all we have about the far-flung telepathic and clairvoyant abilities of some gifted sensitives. The case looks like communication with the deceased.

Whether this holds true with any other specific cases is hard to decide. Before accepting that a medium is truly bearing a message from a post-mortem self, one needs to rule out fraud and also telepathy between the medium and other living people. Apart from mediums, let us note that one out of four Americans believes he or she has had some contact with the dead, according to a national opinion poll.[5] As for a plausibility judgment, perhaps a neutral stance is best in this area at present.

A further area for exploration is the reports of deathbed experiences that suggest an afterlife. Two psychologists, Karlis Osis and Erlendur Haraldsson, have conducted an extensive survey of deathbed visions, as reported by attending physicians and nurses, in the United States and India.[6] In 877 interviews, they found 471 reports of terminal patients who saw hallucinations of persons, chiefly religious figures or dead people. Deathbed visions of surroundings occurred in 112 cases; two-thirds of these locales were said to be other-worldly and one-third were this-worldly.

A more direct set of reports comes from Raymond A. Moody, Jr., a psychiatrist-philosopher.[7] Moody spoke with over three hundred persons who told him they had "come back" after having unusual experiences on the verge of death.

Some of them had been pronounced clinically dead, but later survived. Moody summarized as follows the common elements of typical near-death experiences reported to him: A man (or woman) is dying and as he suffers his worst physical distress he hears the doctor pronounce him dead. He now hears a loud ringing or buzzing and moves swiftly through a long dark tunnel. He suddenly finds himself out of his own physical body; from outside, in emotional turmoil, he watches the efforts being made to revive his body. He gradually becomes accustomed to his odd condition. He finds he still has a "body" but of a different sort. Others approach him. He glimpses the spirits of dead relatives and friends, and a loving, warm spirit of a new kind—a being of light—appears before him. This being questions him, nonverbally, to make him evaluate his life; he sees a panoramic playback of the major events of his life. He then encounters a barrier or border, apparently representing the limit between earthly life and the next life. He finds he must go back to earth, but he does so unwillingly, for he is absorbed by his new experiences in the afterlife and filled with intense feelings of joy, love, and peace. After returning to ordinary life, he tries to tell others of his experience. He can scarcely find words for what happened and, discouraged by scoffers, he falls silent about it.

How much credence shall we place in these accounts? First of all, let us note that Moody's summary fits well with the view of the self developed in our own inquiry. The noise, discomfort, and tunnel-like movement could represent a preliminary wrenching apart of the brain-mind interactive area. The new kind of body, the telepathic communications, and the playback of major memories seem like a foretaste of the postmortem self we have deduced. Our discussion has not posited a "being of light": but such a being fits in easily with our hypothesis.[8]

However, as one reads more of the individual accounts, the question insistently arises: Aren't these the products of imagination, based largely on religious faith or hope, rather than factual reports from a postmortem realm? All the accounts given to Moody derive from memories, and memories often get embroidered in the telling. Moreover, similar states have been reported in nondeath situations. Psychologist Charles Tart found that 44 percent of the 150 marijuana users he studied reported having one or more perceptual out-of-body experiences (like the dying person who looks down at his own deathbed and himself in it).[9] People have also had such out-of-body experiences in exhaustion, emotional shock, fevers, or in excited states induced by dancing or chanting. Visions and communicative experiences similar to those found by Moody, and by Osis and Haraldsson, have been reported also by mystics, mediums, and some ordinary people in states of sensory deprivation. A reasonable judgment might run as follows: The out-of-body experiences may have been hallucinatory imaginings. Most of the other experiences seem suggestive of postmortem reality, but no more fully accurate than the report, say, of a traveler who had been wafted back to thirteenth century Samarkand for thirty seconds and then later tried to tell us about it. Thus they hold some plausibility, but offer no more than meager evidence.

A fourth kind of nonordinary experience involves cases of alleged reincarnation. These usually consist of "remembering" previous lives. Some of these experiences are reported by adults in the Western world. Far more have occurred to children in South Asia, where Hindu and Buddhist thought popularizes the concept of reincarnation, or in other cultures where reincarnation is accepted. The most serious study of these cases has been made by a psychiatrist, Ian Stevenson. By 1973 Stevenson had reviewed about 1,200 reincarnation accounts, of "uneven quality."[10] By 1980 he had offered extended reports on fifty-two cases.[11] These occurred in India, Sri Lanka, Lebanon, Turkey, and among the Tlingit Indians in Alaska. All involved small children who "remembered" another life as an adult elsewhere, that now-dead adult being usually someone unknown to the child's family. This "personation" by a previous personality generally began when the child was from two to five years old and continued for several years before the child stopped talking about it.

Stevenson offers intriguing details in some cases that suggest the reality of reincarnation. However, he also notes the weaknesses of his evidence. All these accounts deal with past events; they depend on interviewing skill and, often, on interpreters; they rely on memories by family members; they are open to fraud ("extremely unlikely") or confabulation or forgetting. Most of all, some form of telepathy with living persons or with postmortem selves might offer a simpler explanation for these cases than positing the invasion of a small child by a complete postmortem adult personality who makes himself known only in the sketchiest way. Stevenson discusses all these issues. He concludes that "for the stronger cases, reincarnation seems to me, as of now, the most satisfactory explanation of them."

John Hick, an English philosopher-theologian, reviewing both theories and facts about reincarnation, proposes for Stevenson's cases an "interim verdict" of Not Proven. "The cases at present available," Hick suggests, "do not oblige us to accept the reincarnation hypothesis. On the other hand they are by no means so weak that we are entitled to ignore them."[12] This is my opinion as well. Here, too, as with the deathbed reports, we may assign a "some plausibility" ranking to the evidence. That is, the positive evidence is meager but, as to these cases, it seems stronger than the negative evidence. We may note also—a point made by Gardner Murphy—that if we accept any of the reincarnation cases as valid at all, they indicate that postmortem memories "necessarily and categorically take a personal form—a self-conscious individualized form."[13] This is what our survival hypothesis asserts. Indeed, some form of limited communication between a surviving postmortem self and the young child may be the most reasonable explanation for these reported reincarnation cases.

Summing up our review of four major types of extrasensory experiences: *Telepathy between the living evidently does occur in some cases. This adds strong plausibility to the idea that post-mortem selves can communicate telepathically. Evidence is hard to validate for the cases of dead-to-living communications, deathbed experiences, and reincarnation. But the evidence for the latter two has at least some plausibility. Insofar as it is valid it fits in with the survival hypothesis.*

23

Some Wider Questions

Our discussion of temporality as the field or ground for human existence, and of the inmost and experiencing self as spread out in temporality, left unanswered some key questions. Temporality as a realm of its own—distinct from, though interacting with, the realm of physical space and mass/energy—offers a home for the inmost self that persists after death of the organism. But this view gives us only a narrow ontology. The whole of reality is clearly much wider than our perspective so far. How does the self-in-temporality view fit into other aspects of reality? We postponed that issue for two chapters, to take up important matters, but now we shall consider it.

Before doing so, let us note that ontology suffers from language problems. The further away one gets from everyday objects and events the less meaningful does our ordinary language become. Ambiguities and equivocations multiply like gnats. One recourse has been to use mathematical equations or logical formulas for theoretical reasoning. These may serve usefully as heuristic devices; but for most of us they lack significance, that is, they fail to link up sufficiently with our store of knowledge and value. Another recourse has been to speak in metaphors and analogies about nonexperienceable or transcendental reality.[1] Metaphors are useful because they are vivid, they may carry a partial truth, and the ambiguities in them can usually be discerned. This is the excuse for speaking at times here in metaphor.

How shall we integrate the extraordinary universe uncovered by science with what we have learned about the human self and its stretching-out in temporality? A first idea runs as follows: Most cosmologists, following Einstein, have used the Minkowski four-dimensional space/time continuum as a locational grid for physical events in the universe. Could we simply accept this, and fit temporality into the time line of the four-dimensional grid? No, that would not work well, because the time line takes time only as succession, while temporality takes time not only as succession but most basically as durational stretching-out. The four-dimensional continuum does notably expand materialistic views of time because it offers a real location not only for the present but also for the past and the future. This is an insight we must affirm. Clearly, too, the time line serves adequately in many notational schemes. But the time line cannot cope with the durational facts of temporality; thus it seems ontologically weak. Perhaps, instead of subsuming temporality under the time line, we should subsume the time line under temporality?

Doing that would give temporality a spread as wide as the whole universe and as long as the remotest past and the most distant future. Quite a jump from temporality as simply the medium or field for being human! To justify such a jump, one might argue as follows: Existents, including the wholly physical ones, can best be considered as systems. An atom is a system consisting of a nucleus circled by one or more electrons, and from this simple system all physical actualities are built up in hierarchies of systems and systems of systems. Now a basic fact about any natural system is that it cannot exist without temporal duration. A hydrogen atom does not consist of a proton plus one electron at a certain spot at one instant of time. No hydrogen atom can come to be unless the electron makes at least one revolution around the nucleus, for the atom only *exists* as a system, and the system only *exists* as an activity, and the activity involves revolutions of the electron. Such a revolution fills a temporal duration, not merely a series of disconnected instants but a durational whole, for without such a whole no system has completed its primal act of existence. The same principle holds with more complex systems, though it becomes difficult to specify just what activation of what essential powers is required for a complex being to come into existence.[2] Since this principle does hold for existence, the fourth (and grounding) aspect of the physical universe, supplementing the three dimensions of space, can arguably be affirmed as temporality (as we have expounded it) and not a simple time line, that is, a mere succession of instants.

To picture this world-view we need a metaphor, and the following one may serve: Imagine a fisherman's net of immense complexity and size. Each knot of the net is a physical thing (system). The strands of the net are vectors in physical fields. The whole of the net is the realm of physical space and all its contents: all that vast universe of galaxies around us, down to the least of physical existents, including also organisms.

Now imagine a great ocean with unknown borders. The net is wholly submerged in this ocean, stretched out in it, moving. The net moves always outward, expanding from the distant central point of its origin. All the ocean behind the net, through which it has traveled, we call the past. The net's current place in the ocean we call the present. Outward in the ocean lies the future, open possibility. This ocean is the realm of temporality and all its contents.

Some of the knots in the net leave deposits behind as they pass through the ocean. These deposits develop what we call innerness or subjectivity. Some thinkers hold that all the physical knots have such an inward side. We have plausibly confirmed such enduring deposits only for those highly complex organisms, ourselves. For humans, we may say that each knot that is the organic or physical aspect of a person makes a kind of node in the ocean as the net moves ahead. This node holds the person's inmost self, extending backward into the oceanic past and projectively forward as well. Some of the ocean's contents, nodal or other, influence the knots and strands of the net as well.

We must picture the great net not as rectangular in shape but as spherical. It is constantly expanding in every direction from its original start at the point (the big bang?) where this universe began. One might think of the net as being like the surface of a balloon that becomes ever more inflated, carrying the whole physical universe on its curving, expanding, permeable skin. But the medium that holds this great net / balloon is not nothingness; it is rather the immense ocean of temporality, stretching from the beginning of time outward to time's unknown end.[3]

Apart from the cosmic aspects of the net / ocean / nodes metaphor, and apart from its individual human aspects, the metaphor also offers a place for history as enduring reality. That is, insofar as historic events are recorded in the inward deposits preserved by the ocean, they persist as a great mosaic of impressions and perspectives—these in addition to whatever written or tangible records remain as physical existents in the present. Likewise, this metaphor offers a possible frame for the durational stretch of various social systems.

Of course the net / ocean / nodes metaphor, like all metaphors, has flaws. Its picture of reality is limited. Thus the net gives a two-dimensional view of the realm of physical space, a realm that is at least three-dimensional in fact. The metaphor leaves dangling various loose ends. It offers no explanation for the experience of mystics who seem to get out of time altogether. Nor does it explain the human thirst for meanings and values above and beyond what people need for practical living. Nor does it locate the source of that light of the mind, or inward light, that humans use. These loose ends are far from trivial. Indeed they can lead us to a new stage in our inquiry, as will appear in the next chapter.

24

Beyond Temporality

What are we to make of the experience of mystics and meditators who enter into a stillness, an emptiness, in which time vanishes? If we allow ourselves an intuitive leap, we shall hazard that the mystics penetrate, in some degree, to an eternal realm. If this be so, what happens to our metaphor of the ocean of temporality, stretching back to the beginning of time and futurally forward so long as time shall last? This would make of temporality a nonultimate level of reality, with an ultimate eternal realm beyond (beneath? above?) it.

That conclusion is, of course, affirmed by mystics themselves. Thus Meister Eckhart held that "God is ever working in one Eternal Now"; and the highest agent of the soul communes directly with God, unconscious of the days, for "in eternity there is no yesterday nor any tomorrow, but only Now, as it was a thousand years ago and as it will be a thousand years hence, and is at this moment, and as it will be after death."[1]

This very old, and persistent, idea that eternity is an unending *now,*[2] a presencing without limit, expands to the utmost (or raises to a new level) the notion we have advanced as to temporality or real duration—that is, its stretching-out, in which a memory of childhood, of youth or of yesterday can all exist and be grasped *together,* in contrast to time defined only as a succession of instants. If we ascribe this inclusive now most basically to eternity, then temporality (with its durational stretching-out) might be a field or medium generated by the impact of physical events upon the ultimate eternal now. Such a view, however, would imply that each inmost self plausibly persists not only in the system of temporality, as we earlier concluded, but also—fundamentally— in the system of an eternal now.[3]

This faces us with two contrasting philosophical views about eternity. Parmenides, originator of Western metaphysics, affirmed Being as an eternal now, unmoving, unchanging, unending:

> . . . Being has no coming-into-being and no destruction, for it is whole of limb, without motion, and without end. And it never was, nor will be, because it is now, a whole altogether, one, continuous . . .[4]

At the end of the Greco-Roman era Boethius, whose description of eternity became the traditional one, held that "the state of God is ever that of eternal presence," in contrast to "whatever suffers the condition of being in time." Boethius defined eternity as "the complete, simultaneous and perfect possession of everlasting life." Such possession "lacks nothing of the future and has lost nothing of the past." Thus God's knowledge "transcends all temporal change and abides in the immediacy of His presence."[5]

By contrast, some twentieth century philosophers of becoming have sought to modify the static view of eternity. Whitehead aimed to do so by positing a consequent evolving nature of God, as well as a primordial unchanging nature.[6] Heidegger, in a significant footnote in *Being and Time,* rejected the "traditional conception of 'eternity,' " taken as a *nunc stans* or standing-now and oriented toward a constant "presence-at-hand." Rather, said Heidegger: "If God's eternity can be 'construed' philosophically, then it may be understood only as a more primordial temporality which is 'infinite.' "[7] Some process theologians, most notably Schubert Ogden, have taken up this idea of the "temporality of God" as a "profound truth."[8]

Earlier, Bergson reacted strongly against static eternity, which he called "the eternity of death"—"an immobile substratum of the moving reality . . . nothing else than the movement emptied of the mobility which made up its life." Instead Bergson advocated stretching out duration more and more, intensifying it more and more, into an "eternity of life." This, he wrote, "would be a living and consequently still moving eternity where our own duration would find itself like the vibrations in light, and which would be the concretion of all duration as materiality is its dispersion."[9] Bergson urged his readers to abandon any "frozen vision of the real" and to plunge fully into real duration.

> And the more we immerse ourselves in it [duration], the more we set ourselves back in the direction of the principle, though it be transcendent, in which we participate and whose eternity is not to be an eternity of immutability, but an eternity of life: how, otherwise, could we live and move in it? *In ea vivimus et movemur et sumus.*[10]

This last, of course, refers to Paul's statement to the Athenians that "in God we live and move and have our being" (Acts 17:28). Indeed it is hard to see how any meaningful personal survival after death is possible without continuing active movement in the inmost self.

A middle view has been offered by the religious philosopher Friedrich von Hugel, who was influenced both by Bergson and by traditional thought.[11] He suggests that *abidingness* exists in a double sense—"an absolute Abidingness, Eternity, in God; and a relative abidingness, a quasi-eternity, Duration, in man (*qua* personality). And the Eternity is always experienced by man only within, together with, and in contrast to, the Duration." This doubling means that "we are indeed actually touched, penetrated and supported by the purely Eternal; and yet that we ourselves shall never, either here or hereafter, be more than quasi-eternal, durational. For only this double sense will save us from the perilous alternatives of an uncreaturely sheer fixity and an animal mere flux and change."

What we find from this short discussion of an eternal now

is that some leading twentieth-century views about eternity (those of some process thinkers, and of Heidegger, Bergson, and von Hugel) cohere well with our own full-life hypothesis of active personal survival after death. This is all that we can hope to achieve. We cannot expect to decide the correct view of eternity. To do so would require, at the least, deep explorations in theology. Our approach has been—and must remain —quite different. Our inquiry began at the empirical level, with an assembling of facts; it sought plausible interpretations of those facts in relation to the notion of survival after death. In a dialectical process, these interpretations were fitted into a generalized picture of the structure and dynamics of the human self. This in turn led us to seek a reasonable ontological grounding for the self in temporality or real duration. That enabled us to deduce what a plausible survival-life might be like, *based solely* on our own naturalistic findings and reasonings. Now, in two further dialectical stages, founded in our progress so far, we have tried to move to a reasonable, though partial, natural cosmology that fits with our findings, and—currently—to use the "loose ends" in our inquiry as stepping-stones to even deeper probings about ultimate reality.

However, at the experiential level the reports about eternity are either very meager (emptiness, limitless abyss) or highly imaginative (accounts collected by Moody, cited in Chapter Twenty-Two, or as a further example, C. G. Jung's visions, cited in Chapter Eighteen). Thus to develop a coherent comprehensive belief about eternity, we stand in need of theological insights, and we shall not try to explore those here. All that we can say about our findings, theologically, is that they cohere with a variety of views about God, that is, about the ultimate explanation and source for whatever is. They cohere as well with a variety of religious faiths. It does seem, though, that various "loose ends" have led us beyond the level of temporality, beyond that durational field or medium in which we humans dwell throughout our earthly lives, and into tentative and partial contacts with something more profound. If this be true, it finally refutes the notion that a human mind (or inmost / experiencing self), if separated from its organic base, would dangle all alone in the universe, a singular and lonely oddity. But the final words on this topic shall go to St. Augustine, who trod the path before us:

> . . . I entered into my inmost being . . . and by my soul's eye, such as it was, I saw above that same eye of my soul, above my mind, an unchangeable light. It was not this common light, plain to all flesh, nor a greater light, as it were, of the same kind, as though that light would shine many, many times more bright, and by its great power fill the whole universe. Not such was that light, but different, far different from all other lights. Nor was it above my mind, as oil is above water, or sky above earth. It was above my mind, because it made me, and I was beneath it, because I was made by it. He who knows the truth, knows that light, and he who knows it knows eternity. Love knows it, O eternal truth, and true love, and beloved eternity! You are my God, and I sigh for you day and night.[12]

25

Where This Inquiry Leads Us

Our goal in this inquiry has been to discover whether a plausible naturalistic case can be made for personal survival after death. Personal survival we took to mean the indefinite continuation of self-identity beyond the perishing of one's organism. We called this the full-life hypothesis. This question is of enduring interest and importance to humankind. Indeed, as we saw in Chapter Two, most human cultures have accepted some form of survival as a fact, though this belief is widely scoffed at today.

Various personal, religious, or metaphysical reasons may lead one to believe in survival or to reject it. In this inquiry we have bracketed out such reasons, without denying their importance. We have instead taken an empirical scientific approach for examining our full-life (survival) hypothesis, using the criterion of plausibility developed in Chapter Three. We have usually used one of two plausibility rankings, along with the comparable negative rankings, in our inquiry: *high* plausibility means supported by a preponderance of evidence that is clear, strong, and convincing: and *moderate* plausibility means supported by substantial evidence that outweighs the opposing evidence.

Substantively, we first considered and rejected as faulty several analytical objections to survival advanced by philosophers. We then turned to the objection that personal identity depends on memory, that memory is lodged in the brain, and that dissolution of the brain at death makes impossible any personal survival. This claim required a long inquiry into whether "pure" memories of individual events and insights (the kind that do largely shape our personal identity) are preserved, and how they might be stored. We examined numerous cases and findings in neurology, neurophysiology, psychology, psychiatry, and phenomenology. We concluded from these that many pure memories do persist and that the brain storage theory of pure memories is highly implausible.

Only by postulating that all memories *must* be stored in the brain, for lack of any alternative, could such a belief be reasonably held. We refused to accept such a metaphyscial postulate. Instead, we proposed that pure memories are stored in the self apart from the brain, and we called this portion of the self the inmost self. The inmost self's linkage to other aspects of the self—experiencing self, foreconscious penumbra, interactive area, organic self—was then set forth in general terms, based on our knowledge of human functioning. While the experiencing self is conscious, we labeled the inmost self superconscious and the interactive area subconscious. We deduced that the subjective I—the part of one that is always a subject, never an object—is most plausibly located in the inmost self, along with one's pure memories. Three great motivating thirsts, somatic, hedonic and noetic, were discerned as shaping the dynamics of personality. The noetic search for meanings, we concluded, is actively pursued by the subjective I, and the whole accumulation of such meanings composes one's personal identity in its inwardness.

By this point in our inquiry, at the end of Chapter Eleven, we began to see the possibility for a kind of survival: When death carries off the organic self with its somatic life-thirst, the whole self might split apart at the interactive level; the experiencing self might then pull back into the inmost self; thereafter, the noetic inmost / experiencing self, with its memories, its knowledge and meanings, its spreading subjective I, might persist indefinitely. But it still remained obscure as to how this survival could take place, as to what does actually go on in the inmost self, and what mode of being it has. Moreover, we still had to face severe objections from some philosophers, that to be human necessarily involves social interaction and that the mind is indissolubly linked to the brain.

On these topics, we noted that human life does involve very strong interactions with the world of nature, society, and other persons. Strong interactions also occur between mind and brain. But we concluded, with at least moderate plausibility, that the inmost/experiencing self is not reducible to or identical with or inextricably dependent on the brain, nor is it merely a cell in the social web or the natural environment. Rather, these strong interactions during life do not rule out movement to a new after-death stage by the inmost/experiencing self. Such movement involves drastic changes, but so does the movement from caterpillar to butterfly, from tadpole to frog, from human fetus to baby.

In Part Three we addressed a further question of great moment: Is the superconscious inmost self merely a passive storehouse for pure memories, or is it active and creative, so that our survival, too, might plausibly be active and creative? We developed three criteria for inmost self activity. We deduced with at least moderate plausibility, that the inmost self is active when one has a conscious experience that derives from unconscious operations, if these operations draw on pure memories, if they seek meanings, and if they help generate useful and novel ideas. Using these three criteria, we found a rich variety of examples illustrating inmost-self activity in thinking, imagining, willing, and judging. Moreover, we uncovered an X-factor at work in these operations, a light of the mind or inward light.

We then examined whether our perceptions are physical things, as they appear to be, and thus could not be preserved as pure memories. In perception we found, on the contrary, an inward, constructed irreducible quality. Thus we discovered that the "paradox of perception," like our other investigations, opens the way to a belief that the meaningful core of being-human is not reducible to brain, organism, or outward reality alone, and therefore may persist beyond the grave.

In Part Four we faced the issue of how anything can exist without a physical basis. More generally, this posed a question raised in Chapter Three, namely, whether the personal survival hypothesis coheres with a defensible ontology. We found that it does so cohere—though without trying to argue that the ontology in question is the only reasonable one. Building largely on the insights of twentieth-century philosophers of becoming, this ontology holds that the field or medium of human existence is temporality or real duration, in which each human self has a real temporal stretch from birth to death. In this view, the organic (physical) self and all its interactions with the physical environment move forward in the temporal present, leaving behind a persistent past (pure memories) and gnawing into the open future (including our futural projections). In this system our mental life, largely in the inmost self, greatly overflows our cerebral life, so that, as Bergson wrote, "survival becomes so probable that the onus of proof falls on him who denies it rather than on him who affirms it."

Building on this approach, and on all of our inquiry so far, we then speculated as to what kind of survival can be anticipated on purely naturalistic grounds. It appeared that survival may be more limited than earthy life in some ways but richer in other ways, and more open both to judgments about one's past life and to a blissful unity feeling. We also reviewed briefly some reports about extrasensory experience, concluding that the strong evidence for telepathy suggests the plausibility of communication among survival selves.

Finally, we attempted to widen and deepen our ontological discussion, without entering into theology. We proposed a world metaphor: the physical universe as a great net moving steadily outwards from an original point, within an ocean of temporality, and each thing-system as a knot in the net, some of which (including humans) make enduring nodes that persist in the ocean indefinitely as inward or subjective systems. We then examined some "loose ends," including the timeless emptiness experienced by some mystics, the human thirst for meanings beyond those of practical life, and the illuminative power cited in Part Three. We found all of these loose ends pulling us toward a realm beyond temporality, toward an eternity that is always now and a source of inward light in which we humans may participate, a source incomparably profound.

We now must render judgment on the great question posed in Chapter One. Has our inquiry made a plausible naturalistic case for meaningful personal survival after death? Let us review the plausibility rankings on the main points in our inquiry:

Purely analytical objections to the survival hypothesis: highly implausible.

Pure memories (and, with them, the contents of our personal identity) are stored in the brain: highly implausible.

Pure memories are stored elsewhere in the self, a locale we label the inmost self: highly plausible.

The subjective I is also located in the inmost self, engaged in the search for meanings: highly plausible.

The rest of the self is organized and operates, roughly speaking, as we proposed: moderately plausible.

Being human is not forever indissolubly tied to social interactions: moderately plausible.

The inmost / experiencing self is not forever indissolubly tied to, identical with, or dependent on the brain: moderately plausible.

The inmost self is an active, creative part of the person, accumulating insights and meanings: moderately plausible.

Perceptions are of a nature to allow perceptual images to become pure memories: moderately plausible.

The personal survival hypothesis coheres with a defensible ontology (though perhaps not the *only* one): highly plausible.

These ten points summarize the principal issues raised in our naturalistic inquiry into the plausibility of personal survival after death. They bear also on the issue of *meaningful* survival, of the kind described in Chapter Twenty-One. What should be our overall judgment as to the confirmed plausibility of such survival?

We note that all of the points are answered affirmatively for survival, with either a high plausibility (supported by a preponderance of evidence that is clear, strong and convincing) or a moderate plausibility (supported by substantial evidence that outweighs the opposing evidence). I believe an overall judgment of moderately plausible is now warranted for personal survival after death, based on the naturalistic grounds we have explored. To claim high plausibility, overall, seems dubious because so many of the points at issue have only moderate plausibility in their favor. It seems clear, however, that the sum of all the evidence opening the way to survival is very substantial, and that it outweighs the opposing evidence. Thus the assertion of moderate plausibility for survival appears warranted.

This inquiry has dissolved any basis for the opinion that survival is a nonsensical idea, a linguistic mistake, a foolish superstition. Afterlife is not merely a possible future for humankind but a plausible one. Our inquiry justifies a belief in survival. It does not, however, oblige or force one to such a belief. It offers no certainty. To obtain such personal certainty one must still look to faith; and there, too, one may find far more detailed picturings of the afterlife than have been suggested here.

Before ending our long exploration, we might briefly consider some differences that a firmly held belief in survival—as developed in our full-life hypothesis—can make in one's living here and now. No doubt the effect of such a belief will differ if one comes into it from faith rather than by climbing up out of a reductionist world view, as happened with me. In the latter case, as one absorbs the full-life hypothesis into belief, along with a foundational belief in the inward light, the whole tone of one's life begins to shift. The sense of boredom, drudgery, meaningless *anomie* falls away. It is as if one had been living in a city with polluted air and then moved to a place with pure air.

In addition to this change, the survival belief may serve also as an emotional safety net. However well we are functioning, moments do arrive when things go wrong. Crises of feeling flare up. We may find ourself treated unjustly. We may be forced to seek a new job, or to consider divorce, or to face life crippled and in pain. We may be assaulted, or we may discover ourself acting shamefully. We may begin to feel crushed, helpless, bereft. In such bitter times, the knowledge that this painful experience is not all of us—that the everlasting inmost self persists, holding the whole core of us since childhood—can help to rescue our consciousness from despair. This, too, shall pass: and our true self remains. We have no need to fear the world, for the world cannot destroy us. Moreover, those loved ones now gone who once consoled us still await us in the end.

Socially speaking, the full-life view makes plain that a person normally is responsible for what he or she has done and will do. Such personal responsibility is required for any rational system of morality, of praise and blame, of criminal justice. Reductionist views cannot provide this. If the individual self is nothing but a material organism, existing only in the temporal present, then the self who did a crime in the past has now vanished: that self literally cannot be punished: and to punish a present self for the act of a now-gone past self is clearly unjust. Likewise, if the self is nothing but a cell caught up in evolution, society, or history, then the individual has no personal responsibility but rather obeys impersonal forces: to offer praise, blame, punishment, reward, is an affair of social or biological convenience merely.

On the contrary, the full-life view with its enduring inmost self implies some responsiblity, some freedom of choice, even in the hardest situations, for normal persons. The fact of this ultimate choice is one of the great glories, and tragedies, of human existence. This can be affirmed and defended coherently only if being human includes a lasting and autonomous inmost self. Without such a self, the phrase "free and responsible choice" has no significance.

Perhaps the greatest insight of the full-life belief is that each human life has a meaning. We humans exist not merely as momentary collocations of atoms, tiny fluxes of mass/energy in a heedless universe, but also as enduring noetic beings in another less alien realm. Moreover, the meaning of a life is unique. It is not duplicated by any other life, for the situation each of us functions in is not like any other's.

Then what is one's life meaning? Psychiatrist-philosopher Viktor Frankl, whose existential psychoanalysis resembles the full-life belief in key ways, offers a notable answer on this. Frankl, who tested his views with his own life in the Nazi death camps of World War II, suggests:

> One should not search for an abstract meaning of life. Everyone has his own specific vocation or mission in life; everyone must carry out a concrete assignment that demands fulfillment. Therein he cannot be replaced, nor can his life be repeated. . . . Ultimately, man should not ask what the meaning of his life is, but rather must recognize that it is *he* who is asked. In a word, each man is questioned by life; and he can only answer to life by *answering for* his own life.[1]

And to whom do we answer for our life? So far as naturalistic inquiry can tell us, we answer primarily to our own inmost self and its subjective I. But that is the self which endures, which outlasts our organism, which seeks meanings, and which eventually will uncover all those meanings —flawed, failed, and sweetly realized—that we have presented to it by living our life. It will uncover those meanings and will judge them, and then go on. But beyond our self there may be a greater, and a loving, and eternal, judge.

Afterword

The mystery of death, the fascination of death, the fear of death: these are the hauntings of our reflective hours. Who shall say—who *may* say—what is to happen when we die? Yet die we all shall, and so long as death constitutes the inevitable end for our physical organisms, our minds will wrestle with the question of survival or ——? No doubt many are like the six-year-old youngster who wrote a letter to God: "What's it like to die? I just want to know. I don't want to do it." Yet, at the end, we all "do it," walking through the door of death alone, the manner of our going a uniquely private *mysterium*.

Religious traditions have generally acknowledged survival as an article of faith. Sometimes that survival is in terms of an aeonic state in which the individual is merged with the Absolute, the "Godhead"; sometimes it is in terms of a "referential immortality," in which the individual survives in the memories of others as well as in his biological offspring. In many religious systems, man is urged to meditate upon death, not as an encouragement to morbidity, but as a reminder that we cannot, indeed must not, postpone our decisions to act meaningfully in the here and now. Tibetan Buddhist texts, for example, suggest that in hesitating to decide on appropriate actions that will fulfill our human condition, we risk the loss of our humanity. The contemplation of death does not point to the futility of life but to its essential importance and value. If survival were not recognized within such traditions, the contemplation on death would serve no purpose.

The reader of Michael Marsh's book will recognize that these religious traditions proceed on a basis different from his empirical approach based on what can be known from experience, experiment, and reason. Marsh's study is remarkably extensive and persuasive, within its modern empirical framework.

It is striking that Marsh's conclusions coincide so well with another tradition, far older than empiricism, which follows its own inherent logic and is founded on its own comprehensive ontology. That tradition—recorded in such texts as the Vedic and Upanishadic literature of India and in the Egyptian, Platonic, Neo-Platonic, and some Gnostic philosophies of the West—proposes, not an inductive ascent from the lowest rung of the ladder of logic, but a descent, as it were. It proceeds deductively from the perception of universal verities and arrives at a recognition of the consequences of such a perception in terms that give meaning and value to human existence. That worldview, called theosophical in our times, includes the undeniable concept of survival.

Of course, the precepts of this perennial philosophy go much farther than could an inductive approach such as Marsh's. The seeker must rely on intuition in this tradition and a sense of the "rightness" of the system as a whole to confirm its verity. Henri Bergson is one among many philosophers, thinkers, psychologists, and even scientists who recognize intuition as a direct, immediate way of knowing, distinct from analytical, representational, rational cognition. Intuition or direct insight is the hoary method of seers throughout the ages. Yet in our days we can hope for more. A methodology such as Marsh's can be thought of as complementing the way of deduction and immediate insight. These two ways of knowing represent opposite poles, not contradictions, and each pole corresponds to an aspect of the human mind. Thus intuition and inspiration can become "grounded" in empirical fact and careful reasoning.

In the theosophical tradition the concept of the "self" is widened and deepened within a context that recognizes the source and origin of all existent beings as an Ultimate Reality, ever-present, boundless, beyond both being and non-being —God. Termed in Eastern literature Brahman—the creative source or ground of all existence as Paul Tillich would term it —that Reality is reflected in the Self or Atman, which again exhibits itself through a myriad of "selves" or separate existences which we come to know as "ourselves." The essential Self is thus indeed immortal, indestructible, beyond the passages of birth and death and their temporality. That Self becomes in turn the "pilgrim soul" of numerous sacred traditions (the "inmost self" of Marsh), undergoing an evolutionary journey in accordance with cyclic law. So the eternal pilgrim, ever surviving innumerable deaths, moves on its way toward the age-old goal of enlightenment. In the course of the journey, that Self becomes the "experiencing self" of Marsh; it takes on the vestures of personalities (the masks of incarnation, including Marsh's "organic self") through which it contacts all the worlds of form in order to develop its own innate divine capacities.

Some traditions, notably the Buddhist, identify the self as simply a bundle of characteristics which, by an inherent lawfulness, must play themselves out on the stage of existence. This doctrine of "no abiding self," as it is often called, recognizes only that continuity or survival which is of the essence of life itself.

Other schools speak of a "higher" or immortal and a "lower" or transient self, analogous to Marsh's "inmost" and his "organic" and his "experiencing" self. His investigations uncovered levels of the self which are surprisingly harmonious with traditional and theosophical views. Going beyond Marsh, the theosophical position acknowledges but *one* Self in which all its numerous expressions are rooted and from which they derive. Just as sunbeams raying into a room through a clear window are not separate from or independent of that central sun which is their source, so all the levels of experiencing selves are not separate from their source in the Immortal Self, the universal Atman. And, as already suggested, within the larger context of the theosophical tradition, that Immortal Self is itself one with its own source, the Absolute or Ultimate, Brahman, the Godhead of Meister Eckhart and the mystics. When the sunbeam disappears because the parent sun has passed behind a cloud, we do not claim the sun no longer exists; so too the deaths of "experiencing" selves do not mark the extinction of the Immortal Self.

From such a point of view dying, as one writer has suggested, is "our most practiced accomplishment," since death is a recurrent episode in the journey itself. The greatest seer of the Middle Ages, Paracelsus, once wrote: "What is death: It is the annihilation of form, not of life. It is the separation of the Immortal from the mortal part of us; it is also that which awakens us and returns to us that which was taken away from us when we were born." Birth and death; death and birth: all species in all the kingdoms of nature shed old forms to renew and perpetuate their kind. Death provides a kind of continuity, the continuity of consciousness, which utilizes forms appropriate to its expanding and growing awareness. The breaking of forms which we call death releases the consciousness within for the new adventure of building other forms for further growth.

The problem of death, then, is ultimately a problem of time, as Marsh points out in his discussion of temporality. Perhaps more accurately, the problem is one of our consciousness of time. How we experience both life and death is determined by how we experience time. Concentration on past and future means that death is painful, a violent wrenching out of context, since what was present yesterday will not be here tomorrow (even though memory, the "pure memory" of Marsh's thesis, does persist). But if our focus is on the flow of time, time as process or as background of process, death becomes one event among many in the temporal flow of existence. In a cyclically ordered world, death is an organic phenomenon; only in linear awareness does a sense of "nevermore" arise. Before human beings had lost the connection with their origins, when man was still in touch with the natural world about him where nothing was conceived as life-less, death was not a contradiction to life, and survival was not in question. The Taoist view, for example, recognizes a total rhythm of life, with a coming forth signifying birth and an "easy parting" signifying death. From such a perspective, death becomes a birth and birth a death. There occurs in consciousness a major revolution in which a spiritual recentering takes place. That which is essential, the "inmost self" of Marsh, becomes primary, and it forever endures.

My personal awareness of this great fact was enhanced some years ago when a very dear friend met death with an equanimity seldom seen. She had been one who had written and lectured about the theosophical worldview, who had wrestled with the great concepts of the meaning of life, the nature of death, the pattern of rebirth, and life's continuity in accordance with law. In the final days of a lifetime given to such work, she spoke of theory becoming knowledge, the ultimate testing of belief in the crucible of experience. And, she said, there is nothing at all to fear; death is release, and beyond its momentary darkness there is light. Death, she knew, is that which makes possible a new birth. And so I knew, as witness, the mystery of death: a dazzling radiance of life in its most blinding moment. Survival? There are only two faces to existence—birth and death—and life survives them both. Just so sunrise and sunset are not essentially different: it all depends on whether one is facing east or west.

JOY MILLS, Director
Krotona School of Theosophy

Notes

Chapter 1

1. *New York Times,* Sept. 12, 1976, p. 25, reporting on a Gallup Poll. The European surveys also cited in this article found a belief in life after death was reported by a high of 48 percent of Italians down to a low of 33 percent of West Germans. Later Gallup Polls show similar results.

2. In *People,* Nov. 24, 1975, p. 67.

3. Richard Eberhart, "The Recapitulation," from Jacob Trapp, ed., *Modern Religious Poems* (New York: Harper & Row, 1964).

4. Viktor Frankl, *The Unconscious God* (New York: Simon and Schuster, 1975), p. 90.

5. William McDougall, *Body and Mind* (Boston: Beacon Press, 1961). p. xxv.

6. Mihajlo Mihajlov, "Thoughts on Society," in *New York Times,* July 27-28, 1971, opp. ed. page.

Chapter 2

1. Cottie A. Burland, "Primitive Societies," in Arnold Toynbee, et al., *Life After Death* (New York: McGraw-Hill, 1976), p. 52.

2. J. G. Frazer, *The Belief in Immortality and the Worship of the Dead* (London: Macmillan, 1913), vol. 1, pp. 27, 28, 24.

3. Burland, *loc. cit.,* p.53.

4. Summarized in Ronald K. Siegel, "The Psychology of Life After Death," in *American Psychologist,* vol. 35, Oct. 1980, pp. 917-18.

5. Geoffrey Parrinder, "Religions of the East," in Toynbee, et al., op cit., ch.5.

6. Severino Croatto, "The Hope of Immortality in the Main Cosmologies of the East," in Pierre Benoit and Roland Murphy, eds., *Immortality and Resurrection* (Herder & Herder, 1970), pp. 22-30.

7. Crispin Tickell, "The Civilizations of Pre-Columbian America," in Toynbee et al., op. cit., ch.4.

8. John A. Hutchison, *Paths of Faith,* 2d. ed. (New York: McGraw-Hill, 1975), pp. 241-42.

9. On these points, see John H. Hick, *Death and Eternal Life* (New York: Harper & Row, 1976), ch. 3. Also Jacques Choron, *Death and Western Thought* (New York: Collier Books, 1963), Book 1.

10. Among the innumerable books dealing with Christian views of eternal life, I shall mention five, for their relevant sections: Hick, op. cit.; Benoit and Murphy, op. cit.: Friedrich von Hugel, *Eternal Life* (Edinburgh: Clark, 1912, 1948); Rufus M. Jones, *Studies in Mystical Religion* (New York: Russell & Russell, 1909, 1970); John Baillie, *And the Life Everlasting* (New York: Scribner's, 1933, 1951).

11. Hutchison, op. cit., p. 463.

12. Lucretius, *On the Nature of Things,* John Dryden, tr., Part III. This and the following quote are from Jacques Choron, op. cit.

13. Marcus Aurelius, *Meditations,* trans. George Long (Mt. Vernon, NY: Peter Pauper Press, 1942), II. 17.

14. McDougall, op. cit., p. xx. McDougall in this book gives a good short history of the spread of the mechanistic view, and also of the rival animistic or teleological views.

15. Bertrand Russell, "A Free Man's Worship," in *Mysticism and Logic* (Garden City: Doubleday Anchor, n.d.), p. 45.

Chapter 3

1. In my dissertation, *Survival After Death: A Philosophical Inquiry* . . . (Ann Arbor: University Microfilms International, 1982), pp. 16-19. Those pages also offer a general discussion of the approach set forth in this chapter.

2. See Edward W. Cleary, ed., *McCormick's Handbook on the Law of Evidence,* 2nd ed. (St. Paul: West Publishing Co., 1972), pp. 793-99, 846. Similar views will be found in Edmund M. Morgan, *Basic Problems of Evidence* (Philadelphia: American Law Institute, 1957), vol. 1, pp. 21-26.

Chapter 4

1. David Hume, *A Treatise of Human Nature.* Selby-Bigge, ed. (Oxford: Clarendon Press, 1967), pp. 252, 253, 259.

2. Ludwig Wittgenstein, *Tractatus Logico-Philosophicus.* Quotations in the text are from 6.431 and 6.4311. Pears & McGuiness, tr. (London: Routledge & Kegan Paul, 1974).

3. See A. J. Ayer, *Language, Truth and Logic* (New York: Dover Publ., n.d.), pp. 35, 117, and *passim.*

4. *David Hume on Religion,* Richard Wollheim, ed. (Cleveland: World Publ. Co., 1964), pp. 269-70.

5. For a broad discussion of this point, see Ian Barbour, *Myths, Models and Paradigms: A Comparative Study in Science and Religion* (New York: Harper & Row, 1974).

6. D. Z. Phillips, *Death and Immortality* (London: Macmillan, 1970), p. 15.

7. Anthony Flew and Alasdair MacIntyre, eds., *New Essays in Philosophical Theology* (New York: Macmillan, 1964), p. 271.

8. Gilbert Ryle, *The Concept of Mind* (New York: Barnes & Noble, 1949), pp. 16, 25.

9. Phillips, op. cit., pp. 5-6.

10. Corliss Lamont, *The Illusion of Immortality,* 3rd ed. (New York: Philosophical Library, 1959), pp. 91, 29, 195.

Chapter 5

1. Bertrand Russell, "Do We Survive Death?" in *Why I am Not A Christian and Other Essays* (New York: Simon and Schuster, 1957), p. 89.

2. Corliss Lamont, op. cit., pp. 62, 77, 76, 78, 79.

3. See, for example, David A. Spieler, "Immortality and Resurrection: A Reappraisal," in *Religion and Life,* Autumn 1974, vol. XLIII, no. 3, pp. 312-24; and Kenneth Vaux, "Intending Death: Moral Perspectives," in *Christian Century,* 1/26/77.

4. "The doctrine that the human soul is immortal and will continue to exist after man's death and the dissolution of the body is one of the cornerstones of Christian philosophy and theology." (*New Catholic Encyclopedia,* vol. XIII, p. 464.)

5. Henri Bergson, *Matter and Memory,* trans. Paul & Palmer (London: Allen & Unwin, 1962), pp. 92-93. A. J. Ayer in *The Problem of Knowledge* (Harmondsworth: Penguin Books, 1956), ch. 4, makes a somewhat similar division that he calls memory of events and habit memory.

Chapter 6

1. In writing this chapter I have used the following sources: Malcolm B. Carpenter, *Human Neuroanatomy,* 7th ed. (Baltimore: Williams & Wilkins Co., 1976): John C. Eccles, ed., *Brain and Conscious Experience* (New York: Springer-Verlag, 1966); John C. Eccles, *Facing Reality* (New York: Springer-Verlag, 1970); John C. Eccles, *The Understanding of the Brain* (New York: McGraw-Hill Book Co., 1973); Gerald M. Edelman and Vernon B. Mountcastle, *The Mindful Brain* (Cambridge: MIT Press, 1978); Philip Handler, ed., *Biology and the Future of Man,* National Academy of Sciences (New York: Oxford University Press, 1970); Wilder Penfield and Lamar Roberts, *Speech and Brain Mechanisms* (New York: Atheneum, 1966); Karl Popper and John C. Eccles, *The Self and Its Brain* (New York: Springer International, 1977); Karl H. Pribram, ed., *Mood, States and Mind,* vol. 1 of *Brain and Behaviour* (Baltimore: Penguin Books, 1969); Theodore C. Ruch et. al., *Neurophysiology,* 2nd ed., (Philadelphia: W. B. Saunders Co., 1965); C.U.M. Smith, *The Brain: Towards an Understanding* (New York: G. P. Putnam's Sons, 1970); Richard F. Thompson, *Foundations of Physiological Psychology* (New York: Harper & Row, 1967); Richard F. Thompson, *Introduction to Physiological Psychology* (New York: Harper & Row, 1975); Paul A. Weiss, "The Living System," in Arthur Koestler and J. R. Smythies, eds., *Beyond Reductionism* (Boston: Beacon Press, 1969). More recent work on the brain, judging from scientific reports, has done nothing to alter the picture offered in this chapter.

2. This has been the standard estimate: however, a leading neurophysiologist, V. B. Mountcastle, has suggested there are about fifty billion neurons in the neocortex alone. See *The Mindful Brain,* p. 37.

3. Handler, ed., *Biology* . . . . p. 328.

4. Weiss, in *Beyond Reductionism,* p. 13.

5. Eccles, *Facing Reality,* p. 20.

6. For a review of these experiments, as they may impinge on our view of the self, see my dissertation, op. cit., Appendix A.

7. Carpenter, *Human Neuroanatomy,* p. 472. Despite the above-cited facts, the thalamus is not a plausible candidate for the central locus of human experiencing. Most of the thalamus seems to be used for communicating with cortical areas, as indicated by degenerative studies. See Thompson, *Foundations of Physiological Psychology,* pp. 101-02, 309-11.

8. See Popper and Eccles, *The Self and Its Brain,* pp. 236-43, and Edelman and Mountcastle, *The Mindful Brain,* esp. p. 37.

Chapter 7

1. Wilder Penfield and Phanor Perot, "The Brain's Record of Auditory and Visual Experience: A Final Summary and Discussion," in *Brain,* vol. 86, pt. 4 (December, 1963).

This 100-page summary includes not only a full discussion but also the full operating room notes on experiential response patients, from which I have quoted below.

It should be noted that spontaneous pre-seizure "dreamy states" have long been reported among some epileptics. Penfield's technique, used at the Mayo Clinic in Minnesota, has also produced some results similar to those found by him and his colleagues at Montreal. (*Ibid.,* p. 685). Some other investigators using similar procedures failed to evoke such memories. (See Paul Fedio and John Van Buren, "Cerebral mechanisms for perception and immediate memory under electrical stimulation in conscious man," paper presented at American Psychological Association convention, September, 1971, quoted in Elliot S. Valenstein, *Brain Control* (New York: Wiley, 1973), p. 110) Much more variable ideational and emotional experiences have been generated by depth stimulation of central brain areas, as cited by Valenstein. Penfield's findings, however, are the most extensive and striking neurological evidence ever assembled about the storage of pure memory.

2. Wilder Penfield and Lamar Roberts, *Speech and Brain Mechanisms* (New York: Atheneum, 1966), pp. 50-53.

3. Penfield and Perot, pp. 688-89. Also, Wilder Penfield, *The Excitable Cortex in Conscious Man* (Springfield: Charles C. Thomas, 1958), p. 38. Penfield and Perot remark: "Complete bilateral removal of temporal cortex has never been carried out. Our evidence would not therefore finally disprove the existence of duplicate records within the cortex of both temporal lobes, but this seems to be unlikely," p. 690n.

4. See Penfield and Roberts, pp. 54-55.

5. Penfield, *Excitable Cortex,* p. 38.

6. In Eccles, ed., *Brain and Conscious Experience,* p. 233.

7. Ibid., p. 275. See also Brenda Milner, "Memory and the Medial Temporal Regions of the Brain," in Karl Pribram and Donald Broadbent, eds., *Biology of Memory* (New York: Academic Press, 1970). She writes: "It seems clear that the hippocampus itself is not the site of the structural changes corresponding to long-term memory." (p. 47)

8. Jacques Barbizet, *Human Memory and Its Pathology,* trans. D. K. Jardine (San Francisco: W. H. Freeman & Co., 1970), p. 154. A later survey article in *Science,* about brain research on memory,

observes that "there is no direct evidence that the hippocampus—or any other brain area, for that matter—is actually the site of storage." Patricia Wallace, "Neurochemistry: Unraveling the Mechanism of Memory," in *Science*, vol. 190, 12 December 1975, p. 1077.

9. K. S. Lashley, in *Proc. Assn. Res. Nerv. Dis.*, vol. 30, 1952, p. 529.

10. Barbizet, op. cit., p. 156.

11. D. Denny-Brown, "The Frontal Lobes and their Functions," reprinted in K. H. Pribram, ed., *Memory Mechanisms*, vol. 3 of *Brain and Behaviour* (Baltimore: Penguin Books, 1969), pp. 390-91.

12. Wilder Penfield and Theodore Rasmussen, *The Cerebral Cortex of Man* (New York: Macmillan Co., 1957), p. 194.

13. Donald O. Hebb, "Intelligence, Brain Function and the Theory of Mind," in *Brain*, vol. 82 (1959), p. 263.

14. Loc. cit., pp. 395-96.

15. For a brief discussion, see Eccles, ed., *Brain and Conscious Experience*, p. 328. Electro-shock treatment may impair long-term memory temporarily and this impairment especially affects memories one to three years old. Larry R. Squire and others, "Retrograde Amnesia: Temporal Gradient in Very Long Term Memory Following Electroconvulsive Therapy," in *Science*, vol. 187, 10 January 1975, p. 78.

16. Ralph W. Gerard, "What Is Memory?" in *Scientific American*, vol. 189 (1953), p. 124.

Chapter 8

1. A third, or dynamic, type of theory claims that memory is held in reverberatory neuronal circuits. Such a process may well take place for a short time, as a perceptual reinforcement. But it doesn't carry longer term memories. Various animal experiments cited by Gerard have clearly demonstrated this fact. See Ralph W. Gerard, in *Scientific American*, loc. cit., pp. 121-22.

2. E. Roy John, "Switchboard vs. Statistical Theories of Learning and Memory," in *Science*, vol. 177, 8 September 1972, pp. 850-53. Also, E. Roy John, "Multipotentiality: A Statistical Theory of Brain Function—Evidence and Implications," in Julian M. Davidson and Richard J. Davidson, eds., *The Psychobiology of Consciousness* (New York: Plenum, 1980), p. 131.

3. A classic experiment in "reconstructive" memory was reported in F. C. Bartlett, *Remembering* (Cambridge: Cambridge University Press, 1967). For recent psychological summaries in this area, see Robert W. Weisberg, *Memory, Thought and Behavior* (New York: Oxford University Press, 1980), especially chapter 3, and John R.

Anderson, *Cognitive Psychology and Its Implications* (San Francisco: W. H. Freeman & Co., 1980), especially chapter 7. Most of the very extensive psychological work on memory in recent years seems rather tangential to our concerns here.

4. Cited by David Rapaport, *Emotions and Memory* (New York: International Universities Press, 1971), p. 252.

5. Cited by F. L. Marcuse, *Hypnosis: Fact and Fiction* (Baltimore: Penguin Books, 1959), p. 100.

6. Robert M. True, "Experimental Control in Hypnotic Age Regression," in *Science,* vol. 110, 1949, pp. 583-84.

7. Ernest Hilgard, *The Experience of Hypnosis* (New York: Harcourt Brace & World, 1968), p. 165. See also Robert Reiff and Martin Scheerer, *Memory and Hypnotic Age Regression* (New York: International Universities Press, 1970), p. 193.

8. Ian M. L. Hunter, *Memory* (Baltimore: Penguin Books, 1964), p. 164.

9. Silvan Tomkins, "A Theory of Memory," in J. S. Antrobus, ed., *Cognition and Affect* (Boston: Little, Brown, 1970), p. 88.

10. Ulric Neisser, "Visual Imagery as Process and as Experience," in Antrobus, ed., op. cit., p. 166.

11. Freud quote is from his *Works,* trans. and ed. James Strachey (London: Hogarth Press), vol. 6, p. 247n.

Chapter 9

1. Edmund Husserl, *Analysen zur Passiven Synthesis,* Husserliana XI (The Hague: Nijhoff, 1966), p. 309, quoted in Robert Sokolowski, *Husserlian Meditations* (Evanston: Northwestern Univ. Press, 1974), p. 149.

2. William James, *The Principles of Psychology,* vol. 1, p. 649.

3. Sokolowski, op. cit., p. 36.

4. Erwin Straus, *Phenomenological Psychology,* (New York: Basic Books, 1966) p. 66.

5. Eugene Minkowski, *Lived Time,* trans. Nancy Metzel (Evanston: Northwestern University Press, 1970), p. 153.

6. These patterns are also interlinked with our pure image memories. A leading cognitive psychologist observes: "Images and propositional information must coexist (in memory). It must be possible to refer to images through words, through inferences. It must be possible to construct new images from parts of old images, to make inferences, to have images organized in such a way that appropriate ones can be found when they are needed." Donald A. Norman, *Learning and Memory* (San Francisco: W. H. Freeman & Co., 1982), p. 64.

Chapter 10

1. *Phaedrus,* 246b, 253d, trans. Jowett.

2. Henry Murray et al., *Explorations in Personality* (New York: Oxford University Press, 1938).

3. B. F. Skinner, *Beyond Freedom and Dignity* (New York: Bantam/Vintage, 1971), p. 189 *et passim.*

4. The phrase *physical realm* is used in the ordinary sense, without attempting to judge whether this realm does or does not form part of an objectively ideal or panpsychic universe. The diagram of Fig. 2 does, however, imply that the self holds something more than the physical: this conclusion is based on our investigations of memory and on the discussion later in this chapter.

5. This part resembles in several respects the diagram offered by the Italian psychiatrist Roberto Assagioli in his *Psychosynthesis* (New York: Viking Press, 1965, 1971), p. 17; though mine also differs from his in several ways.

No attempt has been made to define consciousness in the text. Like personal time, it needs an ostensive definition. The sense in which we are using the word is this: I am conscious when I am aware of experiencing. For a thoughtful discussion, see C. O. Evans, *The Subject of Consciousness* (New York: Humanities Press, 1970). Being aware isn't limited to reflective or self-conscious awareness. I am conscious if I am aware of experiencing anything at all—a percept, a feeling, an image or (at the borderline) simply empty awaiting.

6. Freudians will note that this structuring of the self splits what Freud calls the unconscious into separate subconscious and superconscious areas. This is why: Freud described the unconscious id as "a chaos, a cauldron full of seething excitations" caused by strivings to fulfill instinctual needs. At the same time, he said, the id contains all our old memories. But surely our pure memories could not survive long in a seething emotional cauldron. It seems more plausible to locate our hidden emotional strivings in the subconscious interactive area and our pure memories in the superconscious inmost self.

Working in a different tradition, Maritain distinguishes two kinds of unconscious in a way somewhat but not wholly similar to our distinction between the subconscious and superconscious. See Jacques Maritain, *Creative Intuition in Art and Poetry* (Princeton: Princeton University Press, 1953), pp. 91-94, 106-11.

7. Eccles, *Facing Reality,* p. 56.

8. By speech I mean vocalization of words and by writing the inscription of words. The ideations expressed by these means usually occur, I think, in the inmost self. So, too, with any ideations behind the other skill programs mentioned here.

Chapter 11

1. *De Anima,* 412a, 415a.
2. Charles Sherrington, *Man on His Nature* (Garden City, N.Y.: Doubleday Anchor Books, 1955), pp. 166-67.
3. Paul D. MacLean, "The Paranoid Streak in Man," in Koestler and Smythies, eds., *Beyond Reductionism,* op. cit., p. 263. MacLean adds: "On the basis of behavioral observations of ethologists, it may be inferred that the reptilian brain programs stereotyped behaviors according to instructions based on ancestral learning and ancestral memories . . . The reptilian brain seems to be a slave to precedent."
4. MacLean, loc. cit., pp. 269-70.
5. Quoted by Calvin Hall and Gardner Lindzey, *Theories of Personality* (New York: Wiley, 1957), p. 180.
6. It is worth recalling Freud's observations about the conscious nature of feelings and emotions, since psychoanalysts and others tend to ignore this fact. He made these comments in his 1915 essay on "The Unconscious" (vol. 14, pp. 177-78 in the Standard Edition of his *Works*): "It is surely of the essence of an emotion that we should be aware of it, i.e., that it should become known to consciousness. Thus the possibility of the attribute of unconsciousness would be completely excluded as far as emotions, feelings, and affects are concerned. But in psychoanalytic practice we are accustomed to speak of unconscious love, hate, anger, etc." This properly refers only to repression of the *idea* of the affect, not the affect itself, he writes: "Strictly speaking, then . . . there are no unconscious affects as there are unconscious ideas."

Chapter 12

1. See reference notes to Chapter Four.
2. See for example Gilbert Ryle, *The Concept of Mind,* and Norman Malcolm, *Problems of Mind* (New York: Harper & Row, 1971). For broader views, one might compare the "three worlds" approach of Karl Popper in *Objective Knowledge* (Oxford: Clarendon Press, 1972), and the systematic metaphysics of Paul Weiss in *First Considerations* (Carbondale: Southern Illinois University Press, 1977) and others of his works.
3. Gustav Fechner, *Life After Death,* trans. H. Wernekke (Chicago: Open Court Publishing Co., 1945), pp. 30-31.

Chapter 13

1. C. D. Broad, *The Mind and Its Place in Nature,* p. 607.

2. Karl R. Popper and John C. Eccles, *The Self and Its Brain*, p. 74.

3. C. J. Ducasse, "In Defense of Dualism," in Sidney Hook, ed., *Dimensions of Mind* (New York: Collier Books, 1960), p. 88.

4. For two expositions of these views, a generation apart, see Gilbert Ryle, *The Concept of Mind*, chapter 1, and Richard Rorty, *Philosophy and the Mirror of Nature* (Princeton: Princeton University Press, 1980), chapter 1. For a view more favorable to Descartes and interactionism, see Hywel D. Lewis, *The Self and Immortality* (New York: Seabury Press, 1973), chapter 2.

5. D. M. Armstrong, *A Materialist Theory of the Mind* (London: Routledge & Kegan Paul, 1968), p. 73. Armstrong's views developed out of those of U. T. Place and J. J. C. Smart.

6. Ibid., pp. 49, 50, 89-90. Italics in original.

7. Ibid., p. 58.

8. Armstrong's formula has some plausibility for a limited number of beliefs, which are apt-to-evoke instinctive or habitual schemata; thus, belief in approaching danger may evoke instinctive fight-or-flight response, and belief in the need to get up and dressed may evoke habitual skills to put on garments, button shirt, tie shoelaces, all lengthily learned in childhood. But this applies only in a few cases and even there it covers only *some* responses.

9. The same arguments made against Armstrong can be made against the "group-selective theory of higher brain function" advanced by biologist Gerald Edelman, insofar as he claims to reduce perception, memory, consciousness, planning and all "complex cognitive acts" to brain activities. On the other hand, Edelman's theory seems quite a plausible view as to how the brain may operate in what we have called the interactive area, where various complex schemata are developed and used. See Edelman and Mountcastle, *The Mindful Brain*, pp. 94-95.

10. One philosopher of this persuasion, Feigl, has listed ten major problems for brain/mind identity theorists, as follows: 1. Cerebral localization of mental states and functions. 2. Relation of phenomenal spatialities to physical space. 3. Nature of memory traces. 4. The 'specious present.' 5. Recollection of ordered sequences of past experiences, as in music—"how can a brain process at a given time provide a correct simultaneous representation of such a sequence?" 6. Problems of 'quality,' 'fusion' and 'thresholds.' 7. 'Wholeness' (Gestalt), teleological functioning and purposive behavior. 8. Selfhood. 9. Unconscious processes. 10. Alleged findings of psychical research. (Herbert Feigl, *The 'Mental' and the 'Physical'* (Minneapolis: University of Minnesota Press, 1967), pp. 112-15.)

These problems remain as difficult for identity theorists today as when Feigl first listed them in 1957. The kind of interactionist dualism put forth in the present inquiry does answer most if not all of these problems.

11. Timothy J. Teyler, a neurobiologist, describes Sperry's emergent interactionism as "a view that is probably closest to that held by most contemporary neuroscientists." In *Contemporary Psychology,* 1978, vol. 23, no. 5, p. 293.

12. R. W. Sperry, "Mental Phenomena as Causal Determinants in Brain Function," in *Process Studies,* vol. 5, no. 4, Winter 1975, pp. 249, 250, 255. Sperry also published a largely similar paper with the same title in Gordon Globus, Grover Maxwell and Irvin Savodnik, eds., *Consciousness and the Brain* (New York: Plenum Press, 1976). Sperry's view seems close to what Broad called "emergent materialism," which Broad thought a very strong view.

13. Loc. cit., pp. 248, 249.

14. Paul A. Weiss and others, *Hierarchically Organized Systems in Theory and Practice* (New York: Hafner, 1971), p. 24.

15. Loc. cit., p. 250. Sperry reaffirmed his general view—including interpretation of the events of inner experience as "emergent properties of brain processes"—in his Nobel Prize lecture, delivered in Stockholm on December 8, 1981. See Roger Sperry, "Some Effects of Disconnecting the Cerebral Hemispheres, in *Science,* vol. 217, 24 September, 1982, pp. 1223-226, a reprint of that lecture.

Chapter 14

1. On the role of the unconscious, apart from the depth psychologists, an interesting appreciation from the standpoint of experimental psychology is Howard Shevrin and Scott Dickman, "The Psychological Unconscious: A Necessary Assumption for All Psychological Theory?" in *American Psychologist,* May 1980, pp. 421-34. Among philosophers, James ruled out unconscious mental activity, but I think most philosophers now accept the idea. Broad has a good discussion in *The Mind and Its Place in Nature.* MacIntyre, in his little book on *The Unconscious* (London: Routledge & Kegan Paul, 1958) devotes himself mostly to Freud but has some useful general comments. The Goethe quote is taken from Arthur Koestler, *The Act of Creation,* Danube Edition (New York: Macmillan, 1969), p. 151.

2. Erwin Straus, *Phenomenological Psychology,* p. 70.

Chapter 15

1. Robert Pirsig, *Zen and the Art of Motorcycle Maintenance* (New York: Bantam Books, 1975).

2. See Albert Rothenberg and Carl Hausman, eds., *The Creativity*

Question (Durham: Duke University Press, 1976), ch. 2.

3. From Arthur Koestler, *The Act of Creation,* p. 123. Unless otherwise indicated, the stories I quote about scientists' creative thinking are taken from this book by Koestler.

4. See James D. Watson, *The Double Helix* (New York: Atheneum, 1968).

5. Quoted in *The Creativity Question,* pp. 63-65.

6. Quoted in Brewster Ghiselin, ed., *The Creative Process* (New York: New American Library, 1952), pp. 36-39.

7. Jacques Hadamard, *The Psychology of Invention in the Mathematical Field* (New York: Dover Publications, 1954), pp. 37,

8. On Cardan, pp. 122-23. On Galois, pp. 119-20.

Chapter 16

1. Play is omitted. Play in the sense of kidding, joking or fantasizing together might be considered a type of creative imagination. Play in the sense of sports and games draws so much on subconscious schemata that it does not seem primarily imaginative.

Imagination has drawn increasing attention from both psychologists and philosophers in recent years. Two notable philosophical treatises are Edward S. Casey, *Imagining: A Phenomenological Study* (Bloomington: Indiana University Press, 1976) and Mary Warnock, *Imagination* (Berkeley: University of California Press, 1976).

2. Jerome L. Singer, *The Inner World of Daydreaming* (New York: Harper & Row, 1975). The quotes are from pp. 16-25, 55 and 118.

3. Quotations from Ghiselin's *The Creative Process* are as follows: Wordsworth, p. 84; Housman, p. 91; Spender, pp. 120-21; Porter, p. 200; Nietzsche, p. 202; Picasso, p. 60; Ernst, p. 64; Moore, p. 73.

4. Quoted by Hadamard, op. cit., p. 16.

5. Quoted in E. A. Blackburn, ed., *A Treasury of the Kingdom* (New York: Oxford University Press, 1954), p. 132.

Chapter 17

1. William James, *The Principles of Psychology,* vol. 2, chapter on Will. The quotation is from pp. 524-25.

2. Ibid., p. 578.

3. Gordon Allport, *Becoming* (New Haven: Yale University Press, 1955), pp. 49-51.

4. J. C. Eccles, *Facing Reality,* p. 81.

5. Ernst Mach, *The Analysis of Sensations,* trans. C. M. Williams (New York: Dover Publ., 1959), p. 30n.

6. Rollo May, "William James's Humanism and the Problem of Will," in R. B. Macleod, ed., *William James: Unfinished Business* (Washington: American Psychological Association, 1969), pp. 86-87.

7. A. T. Quiller-Couch, quoted in Blackburn, ed., *A Treasury of the Kingdom,* pp. 124-25.

8. This account is taken from a report in *The Christian News Letter,* April 17, 1946, as reprinted in Blackburn, ed., op. cit., pp. 249-51.

9. In speaking of a central willing that may direct a person's life, we go beyond the definition of willing as an act. That act is a coupling of mental objects with assent, aimed at achievement. Such an act may be often repeated in central willing—indeed, it must continue always repeat*able*—but what about the extensive time between these repetitions, what happens to the willing during that time? One might say that the acts of willing have created in the person a disposition. However, the term 'disposition', like the term 'intention,' lacks the implication of thrustful aiming which occurs in willing. Let us say, rather, that such a person has, through central willing, acquired a purpose. The purpose persists in his inmost self, whether or not he is consciously considering it, and his purposing explains much of his activity, so long as he is *able* to renew his acts of central willing.

Chapter 18

1. This account is taken from J. H. Powell, *Bring Out Your Dead: The Great Plague of Yellow Fever in Philadelphia in 1793* (Philadelphia: University of Pennsylvania Press, 1949), pp. 116-29.

2. Immanuel Kant, *Critique of Judgment,* trans. J. H. Bernard (New York: Hafner Publ. Co., 1968), p. 15.

3. 1 Kings 3:16.

4. Jean Piaget and Bärbel Inhelder, *The Psychology of the Child,* trans. Helen Weaver (New York: Basic Books, 1969), p. 98. Also, Jean Piaget, *Insights and Illusions of Philosophy,* trans. Wolfe Mays (New York: World Publishing Co., 1971), pp. 108, 136. Some other psychologists, by rehearsing children as to comparisons and attributes of objects, have been able to move some of them to the conservation principle at an earlier age than seven; but these results don't seem to invalidate Piaget's findings. See P. H. Mussen, J. J. Conger and J. Kagan, *Child Development and Personality,* 4th ed. (New York: Harper & Row, 1974), pp. 314-18.

5. *Meno,* 86b.

6. For Kant, the beautiful is the object of an "entirely disinterested" satisfaction. For him, if "concepts" enter into the aesthetic judgment, the beauty sinks from "free" to "merely dependent." *Critique of Judgment,* pp. 45, 65. For a view closer to mine, see Virgil Aldrich, *Philosophy of Art* (Englewood Cliffs: Prentice-Hall, 1963), p. 98, or the writings of the art critic Leo Steinberg.

7. Bernard Berenson, *Sketch for a Self-Portrait* (Bloomington: Indiana University Press, 1958), p. 20.

8. Quoted by William James, *The Varieties of Religious Experience* (New York: Modern Library, n.d.), pp. 64-65.

9. Berenson, op. cit., p. 18.

10. T. S. Eliot, *Four Quartets* (New York: Harcourt Brace and World, 1971), pp. 15-16.

11. C. G. Jung, *Memories, Dreams, Reflections,* trans. R. and C. Winston (New York: Vintage Books, 1961), pp. 293-97.

Chapter 19

1. See, for example, John C. Eccles, *The Understanding of the Brain* (New York: McGraw-Hill Book Co., 1973), pp. 194-200. Or the following statement from Russell Brain: "The visual cortex is a necessary condition of vision, for its destruction renders the subject blind, but the same is true of the optic nerves. Why, then, do we attach importance to the cortex? Because it is the last anatomical point on the afferent visual pathway of which this is true. But it does not follow that the function of vision is *located* there." Lord Brain, "Some Reflections on Brain and Mind," in *Brain,* vol. 86, no. 3, September 1963, p. 396.

2. See, for example, Ulric Neisser, *Cognitive Psychology,* p. 10 and *passim.*

Chapter 20

1. Ian G. Barbour, *Myths, Models and Paradigms,* p. 165.

2. Stephin Toulmin and June Goodfield, *The Discovery of Time* (New York: Harper & Row, 1965).

3. Martin Heidegger, *Being and Time,* trans. J. Macquarrie and E. Robinson (New York: Harper & Row, 1962), Section 72.

4. Heidegger also, however, affirms that Dasein, in existing, makes room for its own *Spielraum,* that is, its own place to play life-games. (Op. cit., Section 70)

5. J. E. Orme, *Time, Experience and Behaviour* (New York: American Elsevier, 1969), chapter 8.

6. Henri Bergson, *Matter and Memory,* trans. N. M. Paul and W. S. Palmer (London: Allen & Unwin, 1962), p. 184. This book first appeared in 1896. The theme I develop here was treated as central by Bergson in nearly all his major writings, from 1889 to 1932.

7. Cognitive psychologists and modelers of artificial intelligence are actively seeking some ways to describe these fields of mental activity. For a readable recent account, see Donald A. Norman, *Learning and Memory.* As to the dynamics involved, the reader may recall our short discussion of the three "thirsts" in the self, of which the one dominant in the inmost self is the thirst for meaning. (Chapter Eleven)

8. The reader is urged to consider "field", in the usage here, as a non-spatial metaphor. Its meaning is more comparable to our usage in "the field of economics" than in a "football field."

9. My brain of half an hour ago, like any organized physical system in space, occupied a particular place. That place is now occupied by other physical entities, my brain having moved elsewhere. My brain of half an hour ago, having lost any place to be, cannot therefore exist still. Nor can one argue that my brain exists in a tenseless sense. My brain is a physical mass/energy system. For such systems to continue in actual existence over extended periods would mean a constant ingression of new mass/energy. This would violate the law of conservation of energy. Moreover, a mass/energy system cannot be said to exist if it is incapable of making any difference in any state of affairs. My brain of half an hour ago cannot now do anything whatever. Therefore it does not exist.

10. Henri Bergson, *Mind-Energy,* trans. H. W. Carr (New York: Henry Holt & Co., 1920), pp. 70-71. Quoted from "The Soul and the Body," a lecture delivered in Paris, April 28, 1912.

Chapter 21

1. Marcel Proust, *Remembrance of Things Past,* trans. Scott Moncrieff (New York: Random, House, 1934), vol. 1, pp. 34-36; vol. 2, pp. 991-96.

2. The 1909 book was *Contre Sainte-Beuve,* a collection of essays. Cited by G. D. Painter, *Proust: The Later Years* (Boston: Little, Brown, 1965), pp. 120-30.

3. Hywel D. Lewis in *The Elusive Self* (Philadelphia: Westminster Press, 1982) offers some penetrating comments on the subjective I, especially pp. 149, 158, 175 and 184.

4. This "something" is related to temporality and also to the light of the mind discussed in Chap. Eighteen. We shall revert to this in Chap. Twenty-Three.

5. William Wordsworth, "Lines Composed a Few Miles Above Tintern Abbey."

6. David Thoreau, *Journals,* quoted by Anne Fremantle, ed., *The Protestant Mystics* (New York: Mentor Books, 1964), p. 199.

7. Richard Jefferies, *The Story of My Heart,* quoted by Richard Bucke, *Cosmic Consciousness* (New York: Dutton & Co., 1959), p. 320.

8. The unity feeling at times reportedly follows ingestion of a drug. In such cases I suggest the drug acts to lift the interactive area constraints that hem in the experiencing self. This allows direct contact with a basic source, usually very temporary. The same effect may follow dances and other physically exhausting practices used by some ecstatic groups.

9. Sources are: for Tauler, Evelyn Underhill, *Mysticism* (New York: Dutton, 1961), p. 400; for Eckhart, *Meister Eckhart,* tr. R. B. Blakney (New York: Harper & Row, 1941), p. 121; for Ruysbroek, Rufus Jones, *Studies in Mystical Religion* (New York: Russell & Russell, 1970), p. 311, and Underhill, p. 345.

10. See Edwin F. Taylor and John A. Wheeler, *Spacetime Physics* (San Francisco: W. H. Freeman & Co., 1966), ch. 2, sec. 10.

Chapter 22

1. See Upton Sinclair, *Mental Radio,* revised second printing (Springfield: Charles C. Thomas, Publ., 1962).

2. S. G. Soal and H. T. Bowden, *The Mind Readers* (London: Faber and Faber, 1959).

3. See Montague Ullman and Stanley Krippner, with Alan Vaughan, *Dream Telepathy* (New York: Macmillan Publ. Co., 1973), especially pp. 173-74.

4. See Gardner Murphy, *Challenge of Psychical Research* (New York: Harper & Row, 1961), ch. 7. Quote is from p. 273. Three other useful volumes are: J. B. Rhine, *The Reach of the Mind* (New York: Wm. Sloane Associates, 1947), Rosalind Heywood, *The Sixth Sense* (London: Chatto & Windus, 1959), and S. G. Soal and F. Bateman, *Modern Experiments in Telepathy* (London: Faber & Faber, 1954). A sweepingly skeptical view is presented in D. H. Rawcliffe, *Occult and Supernatural Phenomena* (New York: Dover Publ., 1959).

5. The poll, published in 1975 by Andrew M. Greeley, is cited in Karlis Osis and Erlendur Haraldsson, *At the Hour of Death* (New York: Avon Books, 1977), p. 198.

6. Ibid., pp. 50-51 and *passim.*

7. See Raymond A. Moody, Jr., *Life After Life* (New York: Ban-

tam Books, 1976) and *Reflections on Life After Life* (New York: Bantam Books, 1977). Summary from *Life After Life,* pp. 20-21.

8. Incidentally, I developed the present full-life hypothesis and submitted it as a thesis in philosophy in April 1974, two years before I came upon Moody's first book. Thus it seems a happy event that the experiences reported by Moody's informants fit well with this hypothesis.

9. Charles Tart, *On Being Stoned* (Palo Alto: Science and Behavior Books, 1971), p. 103.

10. Reported in *Journal* of the Amer. Soc. for Psychical Research, vol. 67, no. 2, April 1973, p. 131.

11. See Ian Stevenson, *Twenty Cases Suggestive of Reincarnation* (New York: Amer. Soc. for Psychical Research), and *Cases of the Reincarnation Type,* Vols. I, II, III (University Press of Virginia, 1975, 1977, 1980). Stevenson offers a summary "general discussion" at the end of the 1980 volume. My quotation is from p. 369 of that volume.

12. John Hick, *Death and Eternal Life,* p. 375.

13. Gardner Murphy, "A Caringtonian Approach to Ian Stevenson's *Twenty Cases Suggestive of Reincarnation,*" in Journal of ASPR, vol. 67, no. 2, April 1973, p. 127.

Chapter 23

1. See Ian G. Barbour, *Myths, Models and Paradigms,* and Philip Wheelwright, *Metaphor and Reality* (Bloomington: Indiana University Press, 1962).

2. This approach has developed out of the view of Allan Wolter, who discusses the identity of all existents as systems within the context of substance. He proposes that the ultimate elements of physical systems are simple, with "remote" potencies which become active powers only when united into a system. "Since there seems to be no reason why such elementary entities should be given existence apart from some system in which their powers are actualized . . . we can say that they depend on material systems or bodies not only as to function, but also for their *existence.*" Allan B. Wolter, OFM, "Chemical Substance," in *Philosophy of Science* (St. John's University Studies: Philosophy Series, vol. I; Jamaica, N.Y.: St. John's University, 1960), p. 108.

Ervin Laszlo, more broadly, views the universe as a giant matrix evolving in patterned flows, and systems are the "recurrent sets of events which jointly constitute the invariance of the flow." Ervin Laszlo, *Introduction to Systems Philosophy* (New York: Harper & Row Torchbooks, 1972), p. 293.

This invariance in many physical systems—that is, their resistance to invasion—is a notable fact; thus: "An oxygen molecule in air suffers a million times a million collisions every second, but remains unchanged in all its specific properties as an oxygen molecule," Victor Weisskopf, in *Science,* March 14, 1980, p. 1163.

3. I first offered this metaphor several years ago in an article, "Exploring a New World-Metaphor" in *Friends Journal,* vol. 23, no. 2, January 15, 1977. The surface-of-a-balloon metaphor has been used by cosmologists to convey the expansion of galaxies in the universe. See John D. Barrow and Joseph Silk, "The Structure of the Early Universe," in *Scientific American,* vol. 242, no. 4, April 1980.

Recently I discovered that my net/ocean metaphor was used by the neo-Platonist philosopher Plotinus (A.D. 205-270): "The cosmos is like a net thrown into the sea, unable to make that in which it is its own. Already the sea is spread out and the net spreads with it as far as it can . . . " (*Enneads,* IV, 3, 9; from *The Essential Plotinus,* ed. and trans. Elmer O'Brien (New York: New American Library, 1964), p. 137). For Plotinus, the "sea" was the World Soul, not temporality; but the basic thought is so close to mine that it serves to remind us again how little is new in philosophy.

Chapter 24

1. First quote from Rufus M. Jones, *Studies in Mystical Religion,* p. 227; second quote from *Meister Eckhart,* trans. R. B. Blakney, p. 153.

2. The contemporary existentialist theologian Paul Tillich, for example, declares: "It is the eternal that stops the flux of time for us. It is the eternal 'now' which provides for us a temporal 'now.' . . . Eternal life is beyond past, present and future: we come from it, we live in its presence, we return to it." Paul Tillich, *The Eternal Now* (New York: Scribner's, 1963), pp. 131, 114.

3. For the logic of this kind of relationship, see Charles Hartshorne, *The Divine Relativity: A Social Conception of God* (New Haven: Yale University Press, 1968).

4. From Kathleen Freeman, *Ancilla to the Pre-Socratic Philosophers* (Cambridge: Harvard University Press, 1971), p. 43.

5. Boethius, *The Consolation of Philosophy,* trans. V. E. Watts (Baltimore: Penguin Books, 1969), pp. 163-65.

6. A. N. Whitehead, *Process and Reality,* Part V, chapter 2. See also Hartshorne's *The Divine Relativity,* and John B. Cobb, Jr., *God and the World* (Philadelphia: Westminster Press, 1969). I do

not mean to imply that these thinkers subscribe to our full-life hypothesis.

7. Martin Heidegger, *Being and Time,* p. 499.

8. Schubert M. Ogden, *The Reality of God* (San Francisco: Harper & Row, 1977), p. 163.

9. Henri Bergson, *The Creative Mind,* pp. 186-87. See also Milic Capek, "Time and Eternity in Royce and Bergson," *Revue Internationale de Philosophie,* vol. 79-80 (1967), pp. 22-45. Bergson's reference to the dispersion of duration in materiality denotes his idea that duration is diluted as you go down the scale to simpler, more quick-moving entities, until you reach wholly material entities that are purely homogeneous and repetitive. This idea fits well with our discussion of existents as durational systems in the last chapter.

10. Bergson, op. cit., p. 158.

11. von Hugel, *Eternal Life,* pp. 365-66.

12. St. Augustine, *Confessions,* trans. John K. Ryan (Garden City: Doubleday Image Books, 1960), Bk. 6, chapter 10.

Chapter 25

1. Viktor Frankl, *Man's Search for Meaning* (New York: Washington Square Press, 1963), p. 172.

Frankl's views on memory, time and immortality are summarized in an article he published in German in 1947 and in English in 1966 ("Time and Responsibility," in *Existential Psychiatry,* Fall 1966, pp. 361-66, trans. Joseph Fabry) and which he was kind enough to send me after reading my M.A. thesis, *The Inmost Self.*

In this article, Frankl contrasts the flat-life view that only the present really exists and the opposite "quietist" view that eternity—permanent, rigid and predetermined—is the only true reality. He takes a middle position, holding that "while it is true that the future really 'is not,' the past is the true reality . . . . In the past everything is being conserved forever . . . . Everything is written into the eternal record—our whole life, all our activities, our experiences, our suffering."

As for death, Frankl writes, "while it is true that we can't take anything with us when we die, the totality of our life, which we have lived to completion and death, remains *outside* the grave, and outside the grave it *remains* . . . . What remains is the self, the spiritual self."

Index

Aesthetics, 118
Allport, Gordon, 103
Analysis, philosophical, chap. 4
Aristotle, 60
Armstrong, David, 74-77
Augustine, St., 171
Awareness, 147

Barbour, Ian, 133
Becoming, 133-34
Being, 54, 119
Belief, chap. 3
Berenson, Bernard, 119, 150
Bergson, Henri, 26, 60, 134,
   137-38, 141-42, 169
Bessent, Malcolm, 157-58
Boethius, 168
Brain, chap. 6, 13; 61, 62,
   141-42
Brenman, Margaret, 41
Broad, C. D., 72

Causality, 73
Christian, views on survival, 6,
   9, 25
Cosmic judgment, 119 ff.

Creativity, chap. 15; 97-100,
   140

Daydreams, 96
Death, 139. *See also* Survival
Death-bed experiences, 159-60
Descartes, Rene, 74
Dualism. *See* Interactionism
Ducasse, Curt, 73
Duration, 134
Dynamics, of self, chap. 11

Eccles, John C., 28, 58
Eckhart, Meister, 167
Eliot, T. S., 120
Epiphenomenalism, 72
ESP, chap. 22
Eternity, chap. 24
Existence, 140-41

Fechner, Gustav, 67
Feelings, 62, 149-51
Flew, Antony, 21
Frankl, Viktor, 4, 179
Freud, Sigmund, 45, 54, 58, 62
Full-life hypothesis, chap. 25

Future, 139-41

Ghiselin, Brewster, 97

Hedonic level, 60, 62
Hegel, G.W.F., 66
Heidegger, Martin, 134, 135, 139, 141, 168
Hick, John, 162
Hugel, von, Friedrich, 169
Hume, David, 19
Hunter, Ian, 44
Husserl, Edmund, 48, 134
Hypnotic age regression, 41 ff.

Imagining, chap. 16; 140, 148
Immortality. *See* Survival
Insight, 63
Interactionism, chap. 13; dualist, 72 ff., 130, 144; emergent, 77-78

James, William, 50, 102-03
Jefferies, Richard, 150
John, E. Roy, 39
Judging, chap. 18; 148
Jung, C. G., 121

Kant, Immanuel, 111
Koestler, Arthur, 89
Kubler-Ross, Elisabeth, 4

Lamont, Corliss, 22, 24, 65
Life thirst, 60
Light of the mind, 123-24
Logic, 114

Maimonides dream laboratory, 157-58
Materialism, 12, 72 ff., 84
May, Rollo, 106
Meaning, 57, 63, 85-87
Mechanism, 11
Mediums, 158-59

Memory, chaps. 5, 7, 8, 9; "Pure", 26, 31, 35, 51, 63, 83, 85, 130, 137, 144-46; and neurology, 31 ff.; and neurophysiology, 39; and psychology, 41 ff.; and psychiatry, 45; and phenomenology, 48 ff.; cognitive, 51
Merleau-Ponty, Maurice, 134
Methodology, chap. 3
Mihajlov, Mihajlo, 4
Mind, chap. 13; Part III; 130, 142; definition, 87; unconscious, chap. 14; 57, 94, 100, 109; subconscious, 57-58; mental object, 88, 95, 101, 109. *See also* Self
Moody, Raymond, Jr., 159-60
Morals, 117
Murphy, Gardner, 159, 162
Myers, F. W. H., 159
Mystical experience, 12-21, 150-51
McDougall, William, 4
MacLean, Paul, 61, 62

Needs, 60, 61
Newton's law of motion, 151
Noetic level, 60, 63, 123

Ogden, Schubert, 168
Ontology, chaps. 23, 24; 133, 175, Afterword
Orme, J. E., 136
Osis, Karlis, 159

Parmenides, 168
Past, 52, 137-38
Penfield, Wilder, 28, 32, 138
Penumbra, 56
Perception, chap. 19; 144
Person, 70, 149
Phillips, D. Z., 21, 22, 65

Piaget, Jean, 116
Plato, 54, 116
Plausibility, chap. 3; 19, 53, 68, 143, 176-77
Pleasure thirst, 62
Positivism, 20
Present, 136
Proust, Marcel, 145-46

Reductionism, chap. 13; 3, 12, 84, 178
Rehearsings, 97
Reincarnation, 161-62
Russell, Bertrand, 12, 24, 121
Ryle, Gilbert, 22

Sartre, Jean-Paul, 134
Self, chaps. 10, 11; 53, 68, 144, Afterword; definition, 55; structure, 55 ff., 68; organic, 56, 61, 145; experiencing, chap. 19; 56, 61, 136, 139, 144; inmost, chap. 21; Part III; 57, 68, 93, 100, 122, 130, 137, ff.; interactive area, 57-58, 144; subjective, 59; dynamics, 60
Shelley, P. B., 143
Sherrington, Charles, 61
Sinclair, Upton, 154-56
Singer, Jerome, 96
Soal, S. G., 155-57
Social web, chap. 12
Sokolowski, Robert, 50
Somatic level, 60
Soul, 87, 137
Sperry, Roger, 77-78
Stevenson, Ian, 161-62
Straus, Erwin, 50
Subconscious. *See* Mind

Subjective I, 59, 63, 109, 139, 147
Sufficient reason, 84
Superconscious. *See* Mind, unconscious
Survival, after death, definition, 5; summary, chaps. 1, 2, 5; hypothesis, chaps. 3, 21; 5, 22, 53, 64, 67, 83 ff., 130, 172; varieties, chap. 2; 5; history, chap. 2; importance, 5, 177-79; attributes, chap. 21; 63-64, 67, 83, 122; objections, chaps. 4, 5, 12, 13; bodily, 149
Systems, 164-65

Telepathy, 153-58, 162
Temporality, chaps. 20, 23, 24
Theosophy, Afterword
Thinking, chap. 15; 147
Thirst, chap. 11; 146; for life, 60; for pleasure, 62; for meaning, 63
Thoreau, H. D., 150
Time. *See* Temporality
Tomkins, Sylvan, 44
True, Robert, 42

Ullman, Montague, 157-58
Unconscious. *See* Mind
Unity feeling, 150-51

Whitehead, A. N., 137, 168
Willing, chap. 17; 140, 148
Wittgenstein, Ludwig, 20, 66
Wordsworth, William, 150
World-views, 10, 165, Afterword

About the Author

Michael Marsh, a professional writer and researcher, received his Ph.D. in philosophy at Catholic University in Washington, D.C. Among his many accomplishments, he has authored a newspaper column, "Facts in Your Life," syndicated by the *New York Herald Tribune,* served as correspondent for *Business Week,* acted as associate editor for *Labor,* written a satirical novel, served as economic assistant to the Federal Reserve Board. He is a member of the American Philosophical Association, Washington Philosophy Club, World Federalists, Friends Meeting of Washington. Aspects of his research on survival have appeared in *Journal of Phenomenological Psychology, Friends Journal, Hastings Center Report,* and survival was the subject of his Ph.D. thesis.

Additional Quest books—

AHIMSA—Nat Altman
*Peaceful co-existence with all life through the
application of dynamic compassion.*
AND A TIME TO DIE—Mark Pelgrin
*One man's search for meaning in his own life and
approaching death.*
THE CANDLE OF VISION—AE (George William Russell)
The autobiography of the great Irish mystic, poet.
FINDING THE QUIET MIND—Robert Ellwood
How to attain serenity through mental stillness.
THE SPECTRUM OF CONSCIOUSNESS—Ken Wilber
*A transpersonal view of psychotherapies; the nonduality
of spirit; the unique value of all religions.*

**Available from:
Quest Books
306 West Geneva Road
Wheaton, Illinois 60189**